CHANGING PLACES

A

Christian's

Guide

to

Caring

for

Aging

Parents

Betty Benson Robertson

Beacon Hill Press of Kansas City
Kansas City, Missouri

Copyright 2002
by Betty Benson Robertson

ISBN 083-412-0240

Printed in the
United States of America

Cover Design: Michael Walsh

Library of Congress Cataloging-in-Publication Data

Robertson, Betty Benson, 1943-
    Changing places : a Christian's guide to caring for aging parents / Betty Benson Robertson.
      p. cm.
    Includes bibliographical references.
    ISBN 0-8341-2024-0 (pbk.)
    1. Aging parents—Care. 2. Aging parents—Care—Religious aspects—Christianity. 3. Caregivers—Family relationships.
4. Parent and adult child. I. Title.
HQ1063.6.R624 2002
306.874'0846—dc21
2002013248

10 9 8 7 6 5 4 3 2 1

Contents

Acknowledgments

Special thanks to Earl, my husband, for his loving support, invaluable insights, and unflagging confidence.

I also thank Shawn and Sherri, our children, for willingly enduring the adjustments involved in generations living together and for cheerfully helping.

1
Ready or Not . . .
Here It Comes!

Chippie the parakeet never saw it coming. One minute he was peacefully perched in his cage. The next he was sucked in, washed up, and blown over.

The problems began when Chippie's owner decided to clean Chippie's cage with a vacuum cleaner. She removed the attachment from the end of the hose and stuck it in the cage.

The phone rang, and she turned to pick it up. She had barely said "Hello" when Chippie got sucked in.

The bird owner gasped, put down the phone, turned off the vacuum, and opened the bag. There was Chippie—stunned but still alive.

Since the bird was covered with dust, she grabbed him and raced to the bathroom, turned on the faucet, and held him under the running water.

One minute we're seated in familiar territory with a song on our lips. Then a phone call comes: "What are we going to do about Mother?"

Then, realizing that Chippie was soaked and shivering, she did what any compassionate bird owner would do. She reached for the hair dryer and blasted the pet with hot air.

Poor Chippie never knew what hit him! After that, he never sang much but just sat and stared. It's not hard to see why. Sucked in, washed up, and blown over—that's enough to steal the song from the stoutest heart.[1]

Can you relate to Chippie? I can. One minute we're seated in familiar territory with a song on our lips. Then a phone call comes: "What are we going to do about Mother?" Suddenly we're sucked into the black cavern of uncertainty, doused with the cold water of reality, and scorched with the hot air of anxiety.

It happened to me. Seated comfortably in familiar territory, I had a song on my lips. Anticipation of what life would be like if I ever had to care for my parents never even entered my mind. I had no plan for handling these responsibilities.

My parents were in their late 70s. Each time I went home for a visit, Daddy seemed more frail due to his Parkinson's disease. Mother exhibited the initial stages of dementia, which was causing mental regression, and she was frustrated by her inability to complete daily tasks. I couldn't ignore the signals that something was wrong. Ready or not, the challenge of parent care was upon me.

After careful deliberation and intense prayer, I began making arrangements to move my parents in with my family—the best solution for our situation. In the spirit of the moment, my family and I willingly joined the great army of persons caring for aging parents and grandparents. But nothing in our basic life training up to that point had prepared us for the task.

Until then, *ostomies, Foley catheters, duodenum dressings, decubitus ulcers,* and *incontinence* were irrelevant to my life. But they were about to become everyday reality.

Until then, *bathtub safety rails, transfer benches, deluxe portable commodes, folding walkers, flotation cushions, Depends shields, safety vests,* and *ostomy pouches* were unheard-of terms for me and my family. Now, these products were in our home.

Until then, we were free to set our own daily schedule. Now our lives revolved around pills, bathroom needs, doctors' appointments, balancing checkbooks, medical forms, and the myriad concerns involved in caring for a loved one.

If you're reading this book, it's likely that you're either providing care for an aging parent or you sense that the possibility is on the horizon. You're not alone!

My parents will never get old;
they'll never get sick;
nothing will ever change.

Margaret Close and her husband care for both their mothers. One of their mothers lives in a retirement center and requires assistance with her activities of daily living, so they shop for her groceries, pay her bills, do her laundry, and prepare medications so she can take them correctly.

The other suffers with serious health problems and needs help with home repairs, health insurance forms, business affairs, and other activities.

Melody Watkins, an only child, assumed full responsibility for her mother when her mother became unable to make decisions for herself. Iris Edwards is 76 and caring for her 99-year-old mother. The stories are endless.

According to a survey by the National Alliance for Caregiving and the American Association of Retired Persons, an estimated 22.4 million households in the United States—nearly one in four—are now providing care to a relative or friend aged 50 or older or have provided care during the previous 12 months.[2] Other surveys suggest that today's baby boomers—adults born between the mid-1940s and the mid-1960s—likely will spend more years caring for a dependent parent (an average of 18 years) than for their own children (17 years).

Debbie and Jim, for example, are both in their mid-30s. They have been married 10 years and parent three young children. Both had child-rearing training, but nothing in their life experiences prepared them for taking care of Jim's 70-year-old mother. Debbie relates, "We're moving my mother-in-law in to live with us. I can't imagine the adjustments this will mean. I don't know anything about caring for an older adult."

Adult children typically avoid the aging issue by thinking, *My parents will never get old; they'll never get sick; nothing will ever change.* But chances are that you're going to face the possibility of becoming your parents' teacher, monitor, and caregiver. Ready or not, here comes the challenge of parent care!

2
Honoring Parents

Adult children are to honor their aged parents with reverence, care, and support. The practical application is a personal matter and varies in each situation, but the directive remains: *Honor your father and your mother, as the LORD your God has commanded you, so that you may live long and that it may go well with you in the land the LORD your God is giving you* (Deut. 5:16). This mandate occurs in a slightly different form in Lev. 19:3, *Each of you must respect his mother and father.*

Jesus stressed the fifth commandment's absolute nature. He criticized the Pharisees, who abused the religious vows to escape caring for their parents. He labeled those who denied support for their parents as hypocrites, because what was intended for the parents was given to God (Matt. 15:1-9; Mark 7:9-13).

1 Tim. 5:8 says: *If anyone does not provide [handle the maintenance; meet the needs] for his relatives, and especially for his immediate family, he has denied the faith and is worse than an unbeliever.* Providing care for aging parents sometimes necessitates going beyond sending checks or finding adequate housing for them to sacrificing your time, surrendering your plans, and making major adjustments in your life. Providing does not always mean bringing parents into our home, but I believe God means for us lovingly to meet their needs to the best of our abilities.

No matter how inconvenient it may be,
we must help make choices directly affecting
our parents' lives—emotionally, physically,
legally, and financially.

When facing a decision regarding the care of our elderly parents, it's important to make a distinction between what's *inconvenient* and what is *impossible.* We often assert, "Caring for my aging parents would be unworkable, unfeasible, impractical, unthinkable, unmanageable, and totally out of the question." What we really mean is "It would be *inconvenient.*" No matter how inconvenient it may be, the fact remains that we must help make choices directly affecting their lives—emotionally, physically, legally, and financially. The challenge becomes finding what's best for everyone—not only for our parents, but also for ourselves and other family members.

We honor our fathers and mothers because we have received so much from them, including life itself. We owe our parents for all the benefits they offered us in our early development. *Honoring* our parents moves beyond the inconvenience to doing what is right. Is neglect honoring? Is acting only in our own best interest honoring? Is unkind treatment honoring?

The gratitude we feel toward our parents is sometimes tempered by resentment of the shortcomings and imperfections of their parenting style—whether perceived or actual. Honoring our parents, however, has nothing to do with whether or not we agree with the way they raised us or the way they've lived their lives. It doesn't even have to do with whether or not we like them. Honoring our parents entails, rather, not shaming them verbally or minimizing the investment they made in our lives. The writer of Proverbs reminds us, *Do not despise your mother when she is old* (23:22).

As it does in all other areas of our lives, Scripture continues to offer standards for measuring our behavior and attitudes toward our aging parents:

- *Rise in the presence of the aged, show respect for the elderly and revere your God* (Lev. 19:32).
- *Whoever wants to become great among you must be your servant . . . For even the Son of Man did not come to be served, but to serve, and to give his life as a ransom for many* (Mark 10:43, 45).
- *Let us stop just saying we love people; let us really love them, and show it by our actions* (1 John 3:18, TLB).

In our mobile society, adult children and their parents often live many miles apart, and that distance poses special difficulties in staying abreast of the needs of our parents as they get older. But the basic principle remains—God commands us to love and honor our parents.

Children learn to respect their parents when they observe their parents holding their own parents in high esteem.

God's directives are founded in reason and in His perfect order. His established order is for the present adult generation to honor the previous generation and for the children to honor the adults. When God's command is obeyed, the sequence is established, and the positive progression continues from generation to generation.

Children learn from their parents' example. They learn to respect their parents when they observe their parents holding *their own* parents in high esteem. A few months after our son Shawn and daughter-in-law Nayurel exchanged wedding vows, Nayurel's grandmother, who was advanced in years, became too frail to manage on her own. Shawn said, "I didn't even think about the bathroom that had to be shared, the finances that had to be watched more closely, or vacation plans that would have to be altered. Because of the example you and Dad set of caring for our grandparents, I told Nayurel to have her come live with us. We have never second-guessed that decision."

Choosing to Care

When she speaks she cannot be understood. She does not comprehend what I say to her. Someone must help her with all her personal needs. She does not eat but drinks a special formula from a cup. She does not walk.

I have cared for two individuals who fit this description. One was my infant daughter—the other was my aged mother. My baby girl represented limitless potential. My mother represented encroaching death. Still, I made the choice to care for her.

Many others have chosen to care for aging loved ones. Here are three of their stories.

My mother fell and broke her hip. After her initial hospital stay my sister and I took turns caring for her in her home for one-week stretches.

We both had families of our own that included teenage children, and having us away from home every other week was hard for our husbands and children. We decided to bring Mother into our own homes for a week at a time, and this schedule appeared to be working fairly well until Mother's mind began to deteriorate and the weekly move back and forth began to be confusing for her.

We looked into nursing home care for our mother, but the nursing homes we felt good about had no openings, or the ones with space available for Mother looked shabby to us and didn't really smell that great either.

Eventually we decided on a group home that housed several elderly people. We picked Mother up for weekend visits and occasional outings during the week, but each time I took her back I felt depressed and miserable. After a few months my husband and I sensed God's prompting to bring Mother into our home.

I quit my job, and Mother came to live with us. I took her everywhere with me. I'd load up the wheelchair, and off we'd go to the mall or out to lunch, to doctor appointments, and to visit family. Her dementia made for some interesting conversations on some of our outings, but I thanked God for my sense of humor and for the precious time he gave me with my mother. When she died three years after moving in with us, I knew I had absolutely done the right thing, and I thanked God that I could say goodbye to my mother with no regrets.   —A grateful daughter

When my father died, he left behind two daughters, four grandchildren, and his wife of 64 years. My mother had been his chief caregiver during his last years on earth. She was 82 years old and in pretty good health, but her eyesight wasn't good enough for her to drive. The demands of taking care of my father had taken a toll on her energy. I was living in a rented apartment with my mentally retarded adult daughter, Amy. My other daughter was married and had children of her own, and my sister and her two adult children lived in another state.

My mother invited Amy and me to move in with her. I worked full time, became mother's chauffeur, and did the housework, shopping, and cooking. In the evenings we watched television or talked about the one thing that interested her most—the past. She shared wonderful stories of her childhood, her early marriage, and my growing-up years from her perspective.

Mother died peacefully in her sleep several years later. I've never quite figured out if I did her a favor or if she did me a favor. I only know I wouldn't trade that time with her for anything.   —Cynthia

I'm an only child, and I've always been close to Mom and Dad. After I got married, we lived fairly close to my parents. My wife and my children and I always spent birthdays and holidays with them and dropped by for short visits regularly. My dad died about 10 years ago, and we were able to watch out for my mother.

Two years ago my company transferred me out of state. Soon after we moved we started construction on a new house. We added a small mother-in-law suite, knowing that sooner or later Mom would be coming to stay with us. About six months ago she announced that she was selling her home and moving out our way. We tried to get her to move into our home, but she just isn't ready for that yet. She bought a beautiful mobile home not far from us, though, and we're able to pick her up for church on our way there, and we take her to do her grocery shopping and other errands.

I know sooner or later I'm going to be the one making decisions for my mother and taking care of her—as she took care of me when I was a child. I count my blessings that my wife is 100 percent on board with me about taking on that responsibility. I think it gives my mother comfort to know I'll be there for her when she needs me.

—Dave

QUESTIONS FOR DISCUSSION OR REFLECTION

1. The Bible says to honor and respect your father and mother. What do "honor" and "respect" mean?

_____

_____

_____

_____

2. How can you prepare for caregiving?

_____

_____

_____

_____

3. What does old age mean to you?

_____

_____

_____

_____

4. When did you first notice your parents were aging? How did you feel?

_____

_____

_____

_____

5. How do you feel about the possibility of becoming your parents' "parent"?

_____

_____

_____

_____

6. What fears do you think your parents may have?

_____

_____

_____

_____

7. What fears do you have about your parents aging?

_____

_____

_____

_____

8. How can Isa. 46:3-4 be applied to your circumstances?

_____

_____

_____

_____

9. Why is communication between adult child and aging parent so important?

_____

_____

_____

_____

3

"There Is a Time for Everything"

As I was helping Daddy into bed one night, he said, "You begin life with your mother tucking you in. You end it with your daughter doing it!" We laughed, but my heart was heavy. Role reversal is one of the hardest aspects of parent care.

It can feel overwhelming to watch the ones who were your authority figures during childhood become helpless.

You remember helping your two-year-old child pull up his underwear after using the bathroom, don't you? But have you helped your 83-year-old father retrieve his boxers because he was too weak to do it himself? It's different. You think, *Why does this hurt so much?* It's because inside you're still his little girl.

It can feel overwhelming to watch the ones who were your authority figures during childhood become helpless. It causes sorrow and a deep sense of loss to watch them become needy and vulnerable.

When parents start to get older and begin to confront the problems associated with aging, adult children find the roles reversing. Parents suddenly begin to seem more like children—dependent, sometimes demanding, possibly needing more than can be given. The mother and father who nurtured, comforted, and provided shelter now need the watchful tenderness of the child they raised. It becomes the responsibility of the child to care for aging parents.

Change is the one constant of life. Although not always noticeable, it's inescapable. To live is to change. Scripture reminds us: *There is a time for everything, and a season for every activity under heaven* (Eccles. 3:1).

Resisting change is normal for all of us, but eventually life transitions must be confronted. After all is said and done, there are really only two choices regarding change: face it openly and decide upon a response—or be dragged through change in spite of yourself. In her poem

"To My Dad," Barbara Sheffer expresses her inner feelings about role reversal:

To My Dad

Your hands may not be steady the way they used to be;
When as a toddler learning to walk, they held tightly on to me.

Your feet may shuffle when you walk, and so much slower go
Than when they ran beside my bike when I wobbled to and fro.

Your voice no longer carries the volume of paternal concern,
Needed for those lessons I'd determined not to learn!

Your mind may not recall the facts of long ago;
But you remember things about me that I didn't even know!

Your eyes may be a little dim from watching throughout my life—
The struggle into adulthood with all the pain and strife.

You feel you're no longer needed yet you encourage me with pride;
When I share some new accomplishment that makes me burst inside.

Your heart still holds me firmly with gratitude for being there;
When we didn't see eye to eye, I knew how much you cared.

Thank you for the life I've had;
I'm honored I can call you Dad.[1]

Will you face change openly and decide upon a response—or will you be dragged through it in spite of yourself?

As persons begin to age and start to notice the effects the hand of time is having on their physical bodies, they fear losing their independence, becoming helpless, and the loss of control over their own lives that they face with each new disability. It's natural for them and for us to fight the aging process, but it's important for adult children to try to understand what their parents want. Quality of life means different things to the adult child than it does to the aging parent. The adult child worries about a parent's security, while the parent fights to maintain control of life and reduce impending losses.

As roles begin to change, adult children sometimes tend to disregard a parent's way of doing things, trying to impose their own agenda instead. Parents don't need a barrage of nonstop advice. Unless the counsel given is essential to their safety, offer it and leave it for them to decide.

Grasp the partnership concept by making decisions with your parents, not for them. The privilege of deciding for one's self is important, and it's still important to persons who are getting older. There's a fine line between strengthening their capabilities with our support and weakening their capabilities with our interference.

Change is the one constant of life.

When you take on the role of caregiver for your aging parent, here are some ideas that can help bring about positive changes in your new lifestyle.

- Take a critical look at your situation. What is working well the way you're doing it now, and what could benefit from a change? Write down what needs improvement so you can discuss those items with your parent, other family members, friends, or seek input from someone who has been where you are now who can give advice about what worked well for him or her.

- Establish a regular routine to keep things running as smoothly as possible.

- Do as much as time and finances allow toward making your loved one's surroundings pleasant and functional.

- If necessary and possible, avail your loved one of assistive devices such as special eating utensils, specially equipped telephones, or other items to increase independence and safety.

- Evaluate the nutritional needs of your loved one.

- Write down ways you can think of to provide your loved one with intellectual stimulation—and don't forget to do the same for yourself.

- Schedule social activity for you and your aging parent. Have people over to visit when possible, or plan activities occasionally that will get you and your parent out of the house.

- Find ways to streamline your daily activities to make it as easy on yourself as possible. Make a list of things you need to accomplish today when you're running errands, keeping the location of each destination in mind as you're making your list so you're not running back and forth across town.

- Give yourself and your loved one something to look forward to every day.
- Even if you have only a few minutes, renew yourself spiritually daily.

As adult children, it is important to understand, without minimization or exaggeration, the changes that will likely take place during the role reversal process. Marilyn Hamilton expresses the feelings these changes elicit in her poem "Full Circle":

> It seems the roles of parent and child
>> Are reversed during the later years.
> Now it's me giving comfort and care
>> To the one who used to dry my tears.
>
> The hands that helped me take my first steps,
>> Now hold firmly to me as we walk.
> The voice that patiently taught me speech,
>> Now trembles in an effort to talk.
>
> The one whose memory used to challenge mine
>> To learn and remember each detail;
> Now struggles to recall my birthdate
>> And my children's names, to no avail.
>
> I've heard people claim it's not their job
>> To care for their parents who are old.
> They pay someone else to do that task
>> And keep from putting their life on hold.
>
> I contend it's not a sacrifice,
>> But a privilege to be giving;
> To parents who not only gave life,
>> But made it a life well worth living.[2]

As adult children, we need to understand the changes that take place during the role reversal process.

QUESTIONS FOR DISCUSSION OR REFLECTION

1. What is God's grace and how does it relate to caring for aging parents?

_____

_____

_____

_____

_____

2. Read Prov. 23:22 and think about how this verse applies to your life.

_____

_____

_____

_____

_____

3. Read 1 John 3:18. How does this verse apply to you and your aging parents?

_____

_____

_____

_____

_____

4. Are you willing to commit to caring for your aging parents in whatever manner seems appropriate for their individual needs?

_____

_____

_____

_____

_____

4
Dealing with Decisions

"Before Mother's stay in the hospital, she was living on her own and doing fine," a distressed daughter related. "Now her doctor says she'll need constant care." Frequently a call for help comes suddenly, often following hospitalization. Decisions must be made within days and sometimes even hours.

When faced with such issues concerning your parents, pray for God's guidance. In 2 Chron. 20, we read that a vast army was advancing on Israel. *Alarmed, Jehoshaphat resolved to inquire of the* LORD (v. 3). Jehoshaphat spread the situation out before the Lord (vv. 10-11). He humbled himself before God and said, *We do not know what to do, but our eyes are upon you* (v. 12). God replied, *Do not be afraid; do not be discouraged. . . . the* LORD *will be with you* (v. 17).

As you face the overwhelming decisions, spread them out before God in prayer. Trust the Lord to *guide you in the way of wisdom* (Prov. 4:11). *If you want to know what God wants you to do, ask him, and he will gladly tell you, for he is always ready to give a bountiful supply of wisdom to all who ask him* (James 1:5, TLB).

Contrary to popular belief, most persons over the age of 65 live in their own homes or are cared for by family members. Only about five percent of the elderly live in nursing homes.

Everyone involved in the living arrangements for older adults should participate in the decision-making process. The parents are most affected by the decision; whenever possible, they should have the final say. Generally, older people do not want to live with their children but want to be near them. Adult children, grandchildren, and perhaps brothers and sisters should have an opportunity to voice opinions about the arrangements, especially if their lives will be affected. What worked for your neighbors may not work for your family. Do everything possible to allow your parent to maintain as much control over his or her life as possible.

Here are some guidelines to help you think through the needs of your aging parents.

• People do not age identically. Each situation should be assessed independently. Look at your loved one as an individual rather than a stereotypical old person.

- When symptoms of deterioration are recognized and a more structured environment is needed, assist aging parents with making a decision while they still are competent. The adult child may need to clarify issues and give advice. But the privilege of deciding for oneself is important. Your parents have a right to be consulted about their future.

- Take time to listen to what your aging parents have to say. Observe the entire situation by listening and learning about their hopes, fears, anxieties, and plans for the future.

- The goal is for your parents to remain in their own home and be as independent as possible for as long as possible.

- What is right for one family may not be possible or even right for another. Don't base your decisions on someone else's circumstances.

- Anyone considering becoming a caregiver must be able physically, mentally, and spiritually to deal with the challenge.

- If time is needed to make a decision and adequately prepare, arrange temporary admission to a convalescent or nursing home.

- Circumstances change, and caregiving may not be possible indefinitely. A backup plan is a good idea and should include respite care for extended weekends or evenings out.

---

*Do everything possible to allow your parent
to maintain as much control over
his or her life as possible.*

The following steps will help guide your family through the process of developing an effective care plan. Assess what is happening now. Try to determine what the situation will likely be in one year and within three years.

Assessment Plan

1. **What is the dependency stage of your aging parents?**
   ☐ Minimal (physical strength beginning to wane)
   ☐ Partially dependent (others must help)
   ☐ Total dependency (cannot function unaided)

2. **What is their mental condition?**
   ☐ Normal forgetfulness
   ☐ Impairment of mental abilities
   ☐ Loss of intellectual function
   ☐ Aware of self and others

3. **What is their physical health status?**
   ☐ Ambulatory
   ☐ Walker
   ☐ Wheelchair
   ☐ Bed bound
   ☐ Medications:

   _____

   _____

   _____

   _____

   _____

   _____

   _____

4. **What help is needed with activities of daily living?**
   ☐ Eating
   ☐ Dressing and undressing
   ☐ Personal hygiene
   ☐ Light housekeeping
   ☐ Getting in and out of bed
   ☐ Walking
   ☐ Performing medical self-care tasks
   ☐ Writing
   ☐ Preparing meals
   ☐ Transportation
   ☐ Home maintenance

5. **What services are needed?**
   ☐ Speech rehabilitation
   ☐ Physical rehabilitation
   ☐ Aids for visual impairment
   ☐ Hearing aids
   ☐ Home health care (regular visits by a registered nurse, a licensed practical nurse, a home health aide, or a nutritionist)

☐ Homemaking services (designed to help elderly parents with light housekeeping, laundry, food shopping, personal care, and meal preparation. The extent of services provided depends on the needs. Fees vary accordingly.)

☐ "Meals on Wheels" (program available for seniors who have difficulty preparing their own meals or do not have transportation to a grocery store. Once a day, volunteers deliver nutritious hot lunches and cold food for the evening meal to the home.)

☐ Senior citizen center (social and recreational opportunities that can be a fulfilling outlet for older adults who have the energy and abilities to participate).

☐ Transportation program (most communities offer an older adult transportation system for errands and appointments).

6. **What financial resources are available?**

☐ Automobile $ _____
☐ Bank account $ _____
☐ Bonds $ _____
☐ 401-K $ _____
☐ Pension benefits $ _____
☐ Royalty contracts $ _____
☐ Real estate $ _____
☐ Savings account $ _____
☐ Stocks $ _____
☐ Trust deeds $ _____
☐ _____ $ _____
☐ _____ $ _____
☐ _____ $ _____
☐ _____ $ _____

7. **What insurance coverage is available?**

☐ Life
☐ Health
☐ Property

8. **What are the liabilities?**

☐ Creditors $ _____
☐ Debts $ _____
☐ Mortgages $ _____
☐ Property taxes $ _____

9. **Do I really believe that a situation that seems impossible with human resources is simply an opportunity for God?**
   ☐ Absolutely!
   ☐ I'm trying to trust during this uncertain time

10. **In what condition is the primary caregiver's health?**
    ☐ Poor
    ☐ Good
    ☐ Excellent

11. **Will the primary caregiver be able to physically, mentally, and spiritually deal with impending changes?**
    ☐ Yes
    ☐ Probably
    ☐ Uncertain

12. **What support will there be from other family members?**
    ☐ Partial
    ☐ Wholehearted
    ☐ Local
    ☐ Distant

13. **Are parents willing to change their present lifestyle?**
    ☐ Resounding "Yes"
    ☐ Hesitant "Yes"
    ☐ Uncertain
    ☐ Definite "No"

14. **What is the adult child's disposition toward a different lifestyle?**
    ☐ Negative
    ☐ Hesitant
    ☐ Positive

15. **What is the duration of the commitment?**
    ☐ Months
    ☐ Years
    ☐ Unknown

16. **What are the housing choices?**
    ☐ *Staying in own home.* This option works if the individual can perform daily tasks. Privacy, independence, and personal satisfaction contribute to a high quality of life.

☐ *Moving to a smaller place.* A place less demanding for maintenance or more accessible to transportation may be needed.

☐ *Moving to a retirement community.* This arrangement provides integration of housing and services in a noninstitutional environment. Retirement community houses are usually small and built on one floor.

☐ *Sharing housing.* This is an arrangement in which two or more unrelated people combine their belongings, resources, and finances to share a dwelling. Each person has a bedroom but shares the living room, dining room, and kitchen. Shared housing can produce rental income or simply mean an exchange of services. Possibilities for shared-housing partners are a younger couple, a college student, or several elderly people. Compatibility is a primary concern if considering this option.

☐ *Board and care home.* Residential care may be called "adult foster care" in some areas. The home must be licensed in order to operate. Someone lives in the home 24 hours a day and provides services. Quality of services provided in board and care homes varies. If your parents are accustomed to certain cleanliness standards or have other requirements, select a home that satisfies their needs. Before entering into a contract, make an assessment of services offered so that expectations will be met.

☐ *Continuing care retirement community.* Residents contract for services relating to their living arrangement. This can range from independent maintenance to long-term nursing care. Initially the older adult may live in a private unit. Meals may be shared in a central dining area. If health deteriorates, the resident may move to an area within the community that provides assisted living and nursing care. Carefully screen the program and reputation for quality of care. Obtain a copy of the contract. Understand what services are being engaged. It would be wise to seek professional legal advice before accepting this arrangement.

☐ *Living with family:*
  ☐ Adult children and grandchildren move into the older adult's home.
  ☐ Create an accessory apartment from space already available within the house, providing a complete living unit.
  ☐ Older adult relocates in the child's home with living quarters separate yet a part of the home.

☐ Aging parent lives in the home and is assimilated into the life of the family.

☐ *Temporary admission to a convalescent or nursing home* so adequate preparations can be made and time given for an adequate long-term decision.

☐ *Nursing home.* Deciding whether to place a parent in a nursing home is a wrenching dilemma. Prayerfully consider what is best for your parent. Extensively research recommended facilities. Be sure your lawyer reviews any agreement before signing.

Nursing Home Checklist

Visit each nursing home on your list at least once, unannounced, several times if possible. For the best idea of how a home is run, the following times to visit are suggested: Mealtimes, 4-8 P.M., weekends, and holidays.

	Yes	No
I. Building and Furnishings		
Current certificates and licenses on display?	___	___
Medicare/Medicaid approved?	___	___
State inspection report available?	___	___
Free of hazards underfoot?	___	___
Walls clean?	___	___
Walls painted?	___	___
Attractively decorated?	___	___
Well-lit halls?	___	___
Good lighting in bathrooms?	___	___
Sturdy chairs?	___	___
Handrails in hallways?	___	___
Grab bars in bathrooms?	___	___
Exits clearly marked?	___	___
Exit doors with panic bars inside?	___	___
Doors to stairways kept closed?	___	___
Written emergency evacuation plan in sight?	___	___
Ramps for handicapped?	___	___
Atmosphere welcoming?	___	___
Toilets convenient?	___	___
Towels fresh?	___	___
Bedding clean?	___	___

Absence of strong body and urine odors? ___ ___
Barbers and beauticians available? ___ ___
Near a hospital? ___ ___

II. Staff

Administrator have current state license? ___ ___
Neat? ___ ___
Well groomed? ___ ___
Considerate? ___ ___
Working with patients? ___ ___
Not clustered at nursing station? ___ ___
Easy to find? ___ ___
Speak to patients as adults? ___ ___
Call older adults by name, not demeaning titles? ___ ___
Respond quickly to calls? ___ ___
Certified staff? ___ ___
Physician visits every 30 or 60 days? ___ ___
Private physician allowed? ___ ___
Dietitian licensed? ___ ___
Extra staff to help feed? ___ ___
Dentists available regularly? ___ ___
Optometrist available regularly? ___ ___
Social worker available? ___ ___

III. Bedrooms

Open into hall? ___ ___
Windows? ___ ___
Nurse call bell easily accessible? ___ ___
Fresh drinking water at each bed? ___ ___
Comfortable chair? ___ ___
Reading lamp with adequate light? ___ ___
Clothes closet? ___ ___
Drawers for personal items? ___ ___
Free of unpleasant odor? ___ ___
Privacy for personal needs? ___ ___
Decorate own rooms? ___ ___

IV. Residents

Hair clean and combed? ___ ___
Clothing clean? ___ ___
Involved in activities? ___ ___
Lack of listlessness? ___ ___

Restraints used? — —

Comments they make about their care positive? — —

V. Food

Look appetizing? — —

Fresh fruit served? — —

Vegetables served? — —

Served on regular dishes with silverware? — —

Staff assist those who cannot feed themselves? — —

Can residents get food they like? — —

Meals served in attractive dining room? — —

Specific diets available? — —

Variety from meal to meal? — —

Snacks? — —

Ample time given for each meal? — —

VI. Services

Group activities with option to participate? — —

Individual activities with option to participate? — —

Outside trips? — —

Recreational therapy? — —

Physical therapy? — —

Speech therapy? — —

Religious services offered? — —

Adequate laundry system? — —

Resident council? — —

VII. Finances

Deposit required? — —

When patient's private funds are gone, deposit returned? — —

Do patients handle own personal funds? — —

Daily rate figures available? — —

Extra charges clarified? — —

Listing available of what government pays? — —

Information on what supplemental insurance covers? — —

Clear understanding of what must be paid out of pocket? — —

Making a Smooth Transition to the Nursing Home

Admitting a loved one into a nursing home is an emotionally stressful time for everyone involved. Some facilities have a social worker or nurse specialist affiliated with the nursing home who conducts preadmission group sessions for family members. These informative sessions help ease anxieties.

Accompany your parent on moving day. Your loved one will feel more at home in the unfamiliar surroundings if you decorate their new room with family photos, plants, favorite mementos, and other decorative items.

Visit your parent regularly. The presence of family members creates a personal atmosphere and offers reassurance that they haven't been forgotten and that everyone still loves them and thinks of them. Frequent visitation by family members also sends a message to the nursing home staff that they will be held accountable for the quality of care provided and the kindness and respect shown your loved one.

Solving Nursing Home Problems

If a question or problem arises regarding the care of an elderly person, the first step toward resolution is talking to the nursing staff or the social worker. If your questions aren't answered satisfactorily and the matter continues to be a concern, then meet with the nursing home administrator.

Frequent visitation sends the message to staff that you expect quality care for your loved one.

If these steps do not lead to a solution, contact the nursing home ombudsman who serves the community. The ombudsman office works with nursing home residents and families to negotiate a satisfactory resolution to questions or problems. There is no charge for their services. For the ombudsman's address, contact your state's agency on aging.

Sharlene Wade, certified family mediator (solutions@rockbridge.net), says,

Another option is to contact a mediator to assist in resolving your issues. Mediation is negotiation facilitated by a neutral third party who is skilled and experienced in establishing communication between disputing parties in a nonadversarial manner. In mediation, the parties control the outcome and often have a "win-win" result as opposed to having the issues in dispute resolved by someone not directly involved in the situation. This is helpful in preserving relationships and establishing new patterns for future communication. Mediation generally produces a high success rate in achieving a mutually satisfying resolution, and since the parties themselves choose and agree on the resolution, there are favorable results for all concerned. Mediators may be found through your local office on aging, through the court services, or in the phone directory. Many communities have local conflict resolution or community mediation centers where referrals may be sought. Low-cost or income-proportionate mediation services are often available.[1]

QUESTIONS FOR DISCUSSION OR REFLECTION

1. How can prayer help you when dealing with decisions?

_____

_____

_____

_____

2. Why is it important to seek counsel from a godly person when faced with decisions?

_____

_____

_____

_____

3. Why is it important to involve the entire family in the decision-making process?

_____

_____

_____

_____

4. How are older adults sometimes stereotyped?

_____

_____

_____

_____

5
Facing Feelings

"I know I shouldn't feel this way, but . . ."

Although we don't like to admit it, caregivers often utter these words out loud or at least to themselves. Adult children who are experiencing tremendous pressure brought on by caring for their aging parents find themselves caught in an avalanche of disturbing emotions.

Sometimes it's because of the timing of the unanticipated change. The adult child may be struggling to bring up his or her own children, desperately trying to pay college bills, or reaching the peak of a career. Every stage of life has its challenges, and interrupting our own routines to care for aging parents is not something we think about as we're planning our lives.

Adult children experience tremendous pressure when caring for their aging parents.

Even though a high standard has been set to love, honor, and respect one's aging parents, responsibilities become heavy and are added to an already full daily schedule. Negative thoughts with a tinge of self-pity worm their way into the thoughts of busy caregivers.

1. **Check all the emotions bottled up within you right now:**

   ☐ *Anger*—toward the parent who is ill or other family members who are free to pursue their own lives

   ☐ *Anguish*—from being treated like a little child by the parents being attended

   ☐ *Anxiety*—about the future, finances, and lost freedom

   ☐ *Apprehension*—from looking at your parents and seeing yourself in the future

   ☐ *Chronic grief*—when caring daily for someone who is ill but will never recover

   ☐ *Confusion*—of not knowing where or to whom to turn for help

   ☐ *Depression*—because your lifestyle now seems so overwhelming

   ☐ *Fear*—from wondering if a parent's illness will be inherited

☐ *Frustration*—from trying to adequately care for elderly parents while continuing to meet the immediate family needs

☐ *Guilt*—over thinking it would be easier for all involved if the parent just died

☐ *Helplessness*—from seeing the parent's health deteriorate

☐ *Impatience*—in dealing with diet, disposition, and hygiene

☐ *Inadequacy*—which overwhelms with a sob: "This responsibility is bigger than I am."

☐ *Irritation*—because the water faucet is left running; and a favorite chair soiled from incontinence

☐ *Isolation*—from feeling no one really understands

☐ *Pain*—from remembering what it was like before a parent became "old"

☐ *Regret*—from the "if only's"

☐ *Resentment*—from encroachment on time and energy

☐ *Sadness*—when the person you care about is aging at an accelerated rate

☐ *Stress*—when all fibers of strength are taut

Put a circle around the feeling that has the most intensity for you now.

2. **I am** _____ (put in circled word)
   because

   _____

   _____

   _____

   _____

   _____

   _____

   _____

3. **What would it take to make this emotion go away? I would feel better if**

   _____

   _____

   _____

   _____

   _____

   _____

4. **Look at what you listed in number 3 as things that would make you feel better. Write down ways to make them happen:**

   a.

   b.

   c.

Has your caregiving journey already been a long one? Are you shouldering burdens you feel no one else carries? Are you becoming tired and worn out? Do you have nonsupportive family members who don't help you or who see only the inconveniences your new responsibilities are causing in their own lives? Do your challenges outweigh your strength? Has the initial joy of caregiving been lost? Has your world become chaotic?

Say this out loud: *Jesus knows how I feel.* Continue repeating it until it sinks into your spirit and say it out loud whenever you begin to feel disheartened.

Listen as He whispers, *Come to Me, you who are tired, exhausted, and fatigued from carrying heavy loads. I will give you rest and relief* (Matt. 11:28, author's paraphrase).

We are pressed on every side by troubles, but not crushed and broken. We are perplexed because we don't know why things happen as they do, but we don't give up and quit. We are hunted down, but God never abandons us. We get knocked down, but we get up again and keep going (2 Cor. 4:8-9, TLB).

I, the LORD your God, will hold your right hand, Saying to you, "Fear not, I will help you" (Isa. 41:13, NKJV).

I will strengthen you and help you. . . . I will uphold you (Isa. 41:10).

Even though we as humans would prefer quick solutions for our struggles and quick resolution to our problems, God is faithful to develop our character through the trials we face. *Suffering produces perseverance; perseverance, character,* Paul declares in Rom. 5:3-4.

When you feel conflicted emotionally, search your inner motives and attitudes. Once you have experienced and expressed your emotions, reflect: *God, what are You trying to teach me through this?*

---

*God is faithful to develop our character
through the trials we face.*

---

5. **Character qualities I will prayerfully let God build in my life:**
   - ☐ **AVAILABILITY:** Adjusting personal responsibilities around the needs of those whom I am serving.
   - ☐ **CONTENTMENT:** Realizing God has provided everything I need at the present.
   - ☐ **FLEXIBILITY:** Cheerfully changing my plans when the unexpected occurs.
   - ☐ **FORGIVENESS:** Demonstrating Christ's love when someone offends me.
   - ☐ **GENTLENESS:** Responding to the needs of others with kindness and love.
   - ☐ **PATIENCE:** Putting my personal goals on hold; accepting difficult situations without giving God a deadline to make things more to my liking.
   - ☐ **TOLERANCE:** Viewing every person as a valuable individual whom God created and loves.[1]

Be patient! God will work these qualities into a willing heart. Paul was an old pro at handling difficulties. He wrote,

> *I haven't learned all I should even yet, but I keep working toward that day when I will finally be all that Christ saved me for and wants me to be. No . . . I am still not all I should be but I am bringing all my energies to bear on this one thing: Forgetting the past and looking forward to what lies ahead, I strain to reach the end of the race and receive the prize for which God is calling us up to heaven because of what Christ Jesus did for us* (Phil. 3:12-13, TLB).

This Thing Called Love

God's kind of love says, "Even if I don't feel like it, I will do it—because it is right."

Think before reacting. The only person who can make you act in an unloving way is you. You determine the state of your emotions. There are two possible responses in interpersonal relationships: actions and reactions. We cannot control the actions of others; however, we can control the way we react.

If you sense that a bad attitude toward an aging parent is beginning to surface, stop and think about the way you are responding. Are you treating your parent the way you would want to be treated? Remember, the Golden Rule still applies.

Your name may be lost to your loved one in the fog of age and medication, but he or she still cherishes your presence. Situations you may face in caring for your aging parents can be heartbreaking and soul-burdening. But we are reminded in 1 Cor. 13:13, *But the greatest of these is love.*

QUESTIONS FOR DISCUSSION OR REFLECTION

1. What emotions do you feel may be bottled up within you right now?

_____

_____

_____

_____

2. Which of the feelings you are facing right now seems to have the most intensity?

_____

_____

_____

_____

3. How do negative emotions affect you?

_____

_____

_____

_____

4. Which character quality will you prayerfully ask God to build into your life this week?

_____

_____

_____

_____

5. How do you think God wants you to look at your current situation?

_____

_____

_____

_____

6. What solutions are found in Col. 3:12-17 for the feelings that emerge when caring for aging parents?

_____

_____

_____

_____

6

"How Do I Cope?"

The ongoing process of caring for someone near the end of life can continue for years.

For new parents, every waking moment is devoted to the baby, with round-the-clock feedings and constant care. Young mothers and fathers are often physically and emotionally drained due to lack of sleep. Eventually, though, the baby sleeps through the night, and the worn-out parents start to recover.

The ongoing process of caring for someone who is near the end of life involves days filled with pressuring demands and nights of pure exhaustion, and it can continue for years. Just about the time a routine is established and it seems things are beginning to run smoothly, a new crisis occurs.

How do caregivers cope? One important way is by getting your eyes off the daily difficulties and focusing on the big picture of fulfilling God's will. Working with God increases confidence and gives noble purpose to every tedious aspect of caregiving.

Joy is a result of living in God's divine will rather than indulging our own human will. *Moreover [let us be full of joy now!] let us exult and triumph in our troubles and rejoice in our sufferings, knowing that pressure and affliction and hardship produce patient and unswerving endurance. And endurance (fortitude) develops maturity of character* (Rom. 5:3-4, AMP.).

Daily Prayer

The most accessible resource for caregivers is prayer. *Do not be anxious about anything, but in everything, by prayer and petition, with thanksgiving, present your requests to God. And the peace of God, which transcends all understanding, will guard your hearts and your minds in Christ Jesus* (Phil. 4:6-7).

Carving out personal private time is crucial for your survival. Only God can comfort your spirit. He can envelop you with peace in the midst of trauma. *They that wait upon the Lord shall renew their strength.*

They shall mount up with wings like eagles; they shall run and not be weary; they shall walk and not faint (Isa. 40:31, TLB).

Daily Bible Reading

Reading the Bible *is useful to teach us what is true and to make us realize what is wrong in our lives; it straightens us out and helps us do what is right. It is God's way of making us well prepared at every point, fully equipped to do good to everyone* (2 Tim. 3:16-17, TLB).

Paul's testimony was *This is the reason why we never lose heart. The outward man does indeed suffer wear and tear, but every day the inward man receives fresh strength* (2 Cor. 4:16, PHILLIPS).

Deliberately focus your mind on a selected daily scripture. Examine each word or phrase until its depth captures you. Allow the power of the Holy Spirit to transform your life.

For consistent, daily reading of God's Word, a plan should be followed. It will not happen unless you make it a priority. Here are some suggestions.

☐ Some caregivers have found that the Psalms precisely speak to what they are experiencing. This book of the Bible can be completely read in a month by reading a given number of Psalms each day. One method is to read every 30th psalm: Day 1—Psalms 1, 31, 61, 91, 121; Day 2—Psalms 2, 32, 62, 92, 122; Day 3—Psalms 3, 33, 63, 93, 123; and so on.

☐ The adult child caring for an aging parent faces many decisions and unique situations every day. The wisdom of God can be gained by reading one chapter of Proverbs each day. Since the book contains 31 chapters, it can be finished in one month this way. Proverbs was written *to teach . . . people how to live—how to act in every circumstance* (Prov. 1:2, TLB).

☐ Read a portion of Scripture until it is internalized. An entire month could be spent studying the specific commands of God given in James. Extended time could be given to such passages as 1 Cor. 13 and Ps. 119.

☐ The *One-Year Bible* is arranged in 365 daily selections that make reading through the Bible enjoyable.

For consistent, daily reading of God's Word, a plan should be followed.

Scripture Memorization

Ps. 119:11 (TLB) says, *I have thought much about your words, and stored them in my heart.* Regular intake of spiritual food is vital. Digestion comes through memorizing scripture. When God's Word is in your heart and mind, it becomes active within you.

What needs are you facing? Find a related verse. Write it on a self-stick removable note pad sheet or index card. Memorize the verse while blow-drying your hair, washing dishes, ironing, standing in the supermarket checkout line, walking, or waiting at a traffic light.

Focus on Positive Aspects

It's normal to have negative feelings from time to time. And it's easy to dwell on them and let negativity overtake us. It takes effort to concentrate on the positive aspects of caregiving.

As my mother's dementia gradually became worse, she became incontinent and had no bowel control. The first few times I had to clean her after accidents, I felt anger, resentment, and self-pity. I remember thinking, *Why me?* I avoided looking Mother in the eye. But one time I saw her pain-filled eyes and realized that even though she had lost the ability to verbally express her feelings, she was humiliated. I had been so concerned about my own discomfort and displeasure that I had not stopped to think about how difficult it was for her. I asked God to forgive me and help me think positively.

Pray for inner quietness in spite of the irritations.

Caregiving brings many irritations. Pray for God to grant you an inner quietness in spite of the irritations: *the peace of God, which transcends all understanding* (Phil. 4:7). A relationship with aging parents cannot endure without forbearance and flexibility on your part.

The best survival technique you can employ is learning to cope with your new responsibilities. Accept the fact of generations together and understand there will be problems. Your performance may not always be perfect, but you can commit to do your best.

Prayer Partner

Find a friend or extended family member who will promise to pray for you daily. Scripture says, *Two are better than one, because they have a good return for their work: If one falls down, his friend can help him up. But pity the man who falls and has no one to help him up!* (Eccles. 4:9-10).

Accepting Help

God provides strength for the work He plans for you, but not for the work He plans for others to do. Accept offers of help from family and friends. People usually will not volunteer unless they really want to help you. And the outside diversion of having someone help with your normal activities will be refreshing.

Plan for complete periodic breaks from caregiving from time to time. This should not be seen as a desperate effort to escape, but a planned change of pace—a respite, a much-deserved retreat.

Respite Care

The enactment of the Older Americans Act Amendments of 2000 (Public Law 106-501) established an important program, The National Family Caregiver Support Program (NFCSP). Funded in fiscal year 2001, these dollars have been allocated to states to work in partnership with other area agencies on aging and local and community service providers to put into place multifaceted systems of support for family caregivers. Respite care is a specific component of this system. Respite care could include care within the home, an adult daycare center, or even having your loved one spend a weekend in a nursing home or assisted living facility. Respite care benefits not only the caregiver but also the one for whom you are caring. Constant, unrelieved caregiving can adversely affect your physical health and your ability to continue providing care—leaving two impaired persons rather than one.

There is a wide range of respite care services available based upon your unique needs. In addition to helping with the practical aspects of caring for the older adult, it can also provide short breaks to allow you time to attend a doctor's appointment, go shopping, go to church, take a trip, or visit friends or relatives.

Help in locating local respite care can usually be found in the government section of the telephone directory under "Aging" or "Social Services."

Daily Journal

Keep a daily journal chronicling your emotions. Writing releases feelings and can help clarify relationships. Surprisingly, writing in a journal sometimes is more helpful than talking to a friend. A journal never gives advice. It just listens.

Your performance may not always be perfect, but you can do your best.

You can reveal feelings in a journal that you can't verbalize to anyone. Journaling gives you the freedom to air your deepest frustrations, fears, and wishes, and it brings release, insight, and understanding. You need never share your journal with another person unless you want to.

Support Group

If ever you will need an understanding support group, it is now. Networking with others who are in similar circumstances and experiencing the same challenges you are facing can ease your stress immeasurably. If your church doesn't have a support group for adult children of aging parents, consider organizing one.

How to Organize a Support Group

1. Determine the objective with a brief statement summarizing the purpose of the group. The definition of a supportive fellowship can be found in Gal. 6:2, 9-10.

2. Obtain permission from your pastor or the church board to hold meetings in the church facility.

3. Put the following notice in your church bulletin and newsletter: "A support group is beginning for adult children caring for aging parents. If you would like to participate, please come to the organizational meeting [date and time]."

4. Personally invite persons you know who are caregivers.

5. At the organizational session, state the objective. Set a regular date, time, and place for meetings.

6. Determine a format for the regular meetings, perhaps based on the following example:

   a. Open with prayer.

   b. Introduce and welcome newcomers to the group.

   c. Choose a question to stimulate discussion, such as, "What is the one thing that overwhelms you the most as a caregiver?"

   d. Elicit personal responses.

 e. Pray for one another based on the burdens shared during discussion.

 f. Share a truth from God's Word. Scripture should play a central role in the support group.

 g. Choose one person to bombard with affirmation.

 h. Give practical ideas, such as those found in this book.

 i. Occasionally invite special speakers.

 j. Close with a song, testimony, or prayer.

7. At the first session, become acquainted with each other so that honest discussion and interaction can take place.

8. This can be an outreach for your church. Encourage participants to invite friends, neighbors, and coworkers who also are caregivers.

Laugh

Laughter is good medicine. Allow the humor to surface in predicaments you're facing with your aging parent. Not only will it ease the stress you feel—it may also smooth out tensions your parent is experiencing as well.

Enjoying the gift of laughter makes life easier. Jane Brody, a highly regarded writer on health matters, says it is vital to "use the uniquely human expression of mirth to reduce stress, ease pain, and generally brighten one's outlook on life, regardless of how grim the reality."[1]

Solomon said it this way: *A cheerful heart is good medicine* (Prov. 17:22). A hearty laugh can relax taut nerves and ease weariness.

Keep on the lookout for funny things that happen and funny things people say. Share them with your family so that everyone can have a good laugh.

In her book *Laughing Together*, Dotsey Welliver writes, "Laughter is God's gift. It is vital to our welfare. It can help us through the barren deserts in life. A humorous perspective can lighten the load of our daily work and help us transcend some of our trials."[2]

Exercise

Take care of yourself! Make it a priority to maintain a regular exercise program. Plan to get your heart rate up and get some type of physical exercise at least three times a week. When combined with good eating habits, the potential benefits of exercise include increased stamina and strength; restful sleep; greater resistance to stress, anxiety, and fatigue; a radiant appearance; improved mental health; and reduced risk of illness.

QUESTIONS FOR DISCUSSION OR REFLECTION

1. Can you think of ways to carve out personal time to nourish yourself spiritually?

_____

_____

_____

_____

2. There is joy in knowing you are fulfilling God's will. What are some ways that keeping your eyes on the big picture of God's will is sustaining you as you tend to the tedious aspects of caregiving?

_____

_____

_____

_____

3. Jot down the names of friends or family members who you believe will commit to pray for you daily.

_____

_____

_____

_____

4. In what ways do you feel a support group could help you cope with the responsibilities of caregiving?

_____

_____

_____

_____

7

"Sandwich Generation" Suggestions

Walking your parents through new terminology, medication regimens, available home health services, and paperwork can seem like a full-time job.

When her father's first stroke occurred nine months ago, Sharlene suspected his life would be greatly impacted. What she did not realize was the degree to which his stroke would impact her own lifestyle. Sharlene's parents, although aging, had been active and had found ways to rely on one another's strengths to compensate for their individual weaknesses. Living in a neighboring town and visiting regularly, Sharlene had assisted her parents to varying degrees as she raised her young children.

Her mother had experienced a heart attack less than a year earlier and also suffered from rheumatoid arthritis, which impaired her ability to perform general household tasks. Until his stroke, her father had, among other things, cooked meals, done the laundry, and opened bottles and drawers that her mother could not. Suddenly everything changed. The stroke impaired his vision and ability to swallow and also took his voice and ability to communicate. His sense of balance was affected, making walking dangerous, and his underlying health concerns of congestive heart failure and diabetes surfaced.

Within weeks of the stroke, her father wanted to go home from the hospital. The difficult task of modifying the family home to meet her father's new needs fell to Sharlene. But her life became even more complicated when it was left to her to care for her father in his home while also meeting the needs of her husband and children in her own home.

As the weeks and months passed, other health concerns arose for her father and mother, and the need to be with them increased. At the same time, the needs of her husband and children remained constant. There were groceries to be purchased, meals to be made, clothes to be laundered, appointments to be arranged, physical and emotional needs to be met in both households. The demands of her career were constant, and though she was fortunate to be in a position that did not require her to maintain a set schedule, the responsibility to her employer and clients did not ease.

Sharlene's days began very early in the morning with her own housework and getting her children ready for school. After driving them to school, she drove a half hour to her parents' home to begin caregiving duties there. Beyond their housework and shopping, there were services to coordinate and paperwork to complete. She found herself bogged down in insurance forms and the realization that her parents' health problems were draining them financially.

Walking her parents through new terminology, medication regimens, and the available home health services and accompanying paperwork seemed to her to be another full-time job. Taking care of correspondence and completing her career responsibilities during the infrequent breaks from caring for her parents became the norm, and when she was away from her parents she clutched a cell phone.

Sharlene had been unexpectedly ushered into the "sandwich generation." She commented that her sandwich must be peanut butter and jelly. "I'm wedged between the needs of my parents and my children," she said. "Every situation becomes sticky, and what's in the middle is quickly getting squeezed out."

The "sandwich generation" is comprised of individuals caught in the middle between what their children want and need, what they themselves want and need, and what their parents want and need.

Choosing between assisting her parents and attending her sons' school and sports activities is a regular occurrence. Her frustration was apparent when she said, "I feel the need to honor my father and mother, but I also have a commitment to my husband and children. This is not just a difficult week or two out of our lives—it's becoming a way of life. I can't help but wonder how my children see my role. Am I leading by example in showing them my commitment to my parents? Or do they feel cheated by my divided attention? I'm sandwiched between all these people that I love. Beyond that, I feel guilty about wanting time for myself, because I feel that I'm already cheating them out of my limited time. The reality is that I'll never get back this precious time in my children's lives, but I know that the time I have left with my parents is limited too."[1]

Caring for your parents will add to your already long list of daily duties. There will be added demands of playing phone tag with social workers, scheduling doctors' appointments, arranging transportation, paying bills, and holding your breath until the next crisis. If you're facing the unique challenges of multigenerational living, you may find some of the following suggestions helpful.

1. **Use available resources.** All caregiving situations are unique, but the wheel does not need to be reinvented! Numerous resources and shortcuts are available to help you navigate the maze of public agencies, private services, and volunteer organizations.

2. **Hold regular family meetings with all generations present.** Take this opportunity to allow those who are present to air their feelings, consider solutions to existing problems, exchange points of view, and handle complaints. Discuss difficult feelings that may result in blow-ups if not resolved. Communication is vital to a healthy, caring family, especially during this difficult time.

3. **Post a chart to hold family members accountable for changing problem behaviors.** This chart might read: Grandpa promises to rinse his whiskers down the sink after shaving; Grandma will work at saying one positive thing to every family member each day; Lucy will lower the volume on her stereo during the grandparents' nap time; Mother consents to letting Grandma cook one meal a week; Father agrees to putting a weekly date with Mom on his calendar.

4. **Establish an information center near the main phone, and keep a large master calendar there.** All family members should responsibly enter upcoming events and related phone numbers. All handouts with detailed information about activities should be kept in this designated place.

5. **Once a month, "take five."** Allow five minutes to give positive feedback to one another. Perhaps one of these ideas will work in your family:

*Bombardment—Choose one family member to bombard with positive comments. Speak directly to the individual: "Dad, I appreciate how sensitive you are to my feelings" or "You are a wonderful son-in-law. I appreciate the spiritual leadership you give the family."

*Here's my heart—If there are six people in the family, for example, each person gets five white hearts made from construction paper.

Words of love and appreciation are written on the hearts, one message for each of the other family members. Hearts are then distributed.

*Web of love—Family members sit in a circle. The father has a ball of yarn. He wraps the yarn around his finger and then tosses the ball to someone. He expresses his appreciation to that person. Then that person wraps the yarn around his or her finger and then tosses the ball to someone else and repeats the process. This continues until a large "web of love" forms.

6. **Post family rules.** Talk about the rules in a family meeting and obtain input from all family members. Be sure to include eating schedules, cleaning responsibilities, laundry duties, and all other aspects of keeping your home running smoothly. Review the rules occasionally to accommodate changing circumstances and to keep lines of communication open.

7. **Respect the privacy of each family member.** Personal boundaries and personal space should be defined, allowing all generations to have their own lives independent of each other as needed.

8. **Keep the needs of your children a top priority.** Except in extreme emergencies, the household should function as it did prior to the time the aging parents moved in, and regular activities should be continued. This may require locating several trustworthy individuals who will come stay with your parents as needed. Leave the phone number where you can be reached and detailed instructions concerning care of your parents.

9. **Have a weekly date with your spouse away from the house.** Guard your marriage to ensure that it doesn't become a victim to the emotional pressures of multigenerational living.

10. **If siblings or other family members live nearby, share caregiving responsibilities.** Use available help productively, and don't be afraid to ask for help when you need it. When providing care for an older parent, the more help you receive, the better! Responsibilities can be assigned for legal, financial, medical, and other issues.

11. **Contact nonfamily sources for help.** A church teen might be hired to do yard work, a retired person could provide transportation services, and a friend might be able to help run errands.

12. **Read 1 Cor. 13:4-7** (TLB) often, when all family members are present:

> Love is very patient and kind, never jealous or envious, never boastful or proud, never haughty or selfish or rude. Love does not demand its own way. It is not irritable or touchy. It does not hold grudges and will hardly

even notice when others do it wrong. It is never glad about injustice, but rejoices whenever truth wins out. If you love someone you will be loyal to him no matter what the cost. You will always believe in him, always expect the best of him, and always stand your ground in defending him.

13. Apply the Golden Rule. Are all family members treating each other the way they would want to be treated? *In everything, do to others what you would have them do to you* (Matt. 7:12).

14. Plan fun activities to do as a family, such as the following:

＊Indoor Scavenger Hunt/Beat the Clock

- *a.* Make a list of items for the children to find. Be specific—red sock, black comb, box of Wheaties cereal, and so on.
- *b.* Keep track of how long it takes everyone to find these items and how long it takes to put them back in their proper places.
- *c.* Use the same list again. See how long it takes a second time to find the items and then replace them.
- *d.* Keep the list and play again.

＊Indoor Hide and Seek

Playing "Hide and Seek" as a family creates a memory that will last a lifetime. Before starting, sit down together and make a list of rules.

＊Hat Day

Using brown paper bags and scraps of things found around the house, have each family member make a funny hat. Everyone can wear the hat at dinner.

＊Beat the Clock Clean-up

All family members, including parents, clean up their rooms in a certain amount of time.

＊Indoor Picnic

Involve the entire family in fixing the meal. Spread out a blanket on the floor and enjoy!

＊Crazy Olympics

Work together in setting up various events:

- *a.* Discus throw, using paper plates
- *b.* Javelin throw, using straws
- *c.* Shot put, using marshmallows
- *d.* Diving, with each person tossing jelly beans into a container of water
- *e.* One-yard dash, by pushing a marshmallow across the floor with the nose
- *f.* Indoor mile—50 feet with hands on ankles

g. Twenty-foot dash, hopping a given distance on one foot

h. Fifty-yard dash, unrolling toilet paper from one end of room to the other

❊Cupcake Decorating

Make cupcakes and divide them among family members. Provide supplies with which to create, such as icing, sprinkles, M&M's, raisins, nuts, and so on. Each person decorates his or her own cupcake.

❊Game Marathon

Play one round of every table game your family has.

❊Paper Airplane Mania

Create airplanes from leftover school notebook paper. See whose will stay in flight the longest and whose plane is the winner of the distance race!

❊Peanut Hunt

Buy a large bag of peanuts. Toss them into a grassy area in your yard. Give everyone a paper sack. At a signal, start to hunt for the peanuts, dropping them into the sack as found. See who gets the most. The one who got the least amount can scatter the peanuts for everyone to find again. Play until interest runs out; then divide the peanuts evenly and enjoy!

❊Water Balloon Fight

Set rules for the fight. Then fill balloons with water, tie securely, and stack in the designated place. On your mark, get set, throw!

❊Wacky Volleyball

If you don't have a volleyball net, just tie rope or yarn between two trees or take two chairs outside. Use a large beach ball.

❊Balloon Volleyball

Tie a string from one side of the room to the other at about chin height. Play volleyball, using a round balloon. Players over 4'6" must play on their knees! Remove lamps and other breakables before starting.

❊Pizza Party

Make a list of all ingredients needed to make your very own pizzas. Go shopping, and then work together as a family creating individual pizzas.

❊Parent Wrap-Up

Children "wrap-up" each parent using toilet paper.

❊Crazy Contests

Burp—who can burp first after drinking a soda?

Whistle—who can whistle first after eating a soda cracker?

Balloon blow—who can be first to blow up a balloon until it pops?

Bubble gum race—who can blow a bubble first?

Seed-spitting—who can spit watermelon seeds the longest distance?

Kleenex blow—who can keep a Kleenex in the air the longest by blowing on it?

✽Reading Safari

Everyone finds a favorite book, looks for a comfortable place, and reads!

✽Anything Goes!

Use a familiar table game, and let each child make up different rules.

✽Exercise Together

Family members can take turns leading aerobics.

✽Jigsaw Puzzle Challenge

Get a difficult puzzle and work together to complete it.

✽Dramatize a Bible Story

Read a Bible story together and then act it out.

✽Bean Bag Basketball

Place a large container or box in the center of the floor. Toss in the bean bag. Keep points.

✽Cleaning Party

Put on a compact disk that everyone enjoys. Clean until the end of the music—then everyone gets surprise refreshments.

✽Treasure Hunt

Start with a note: "Make your bed. Then read the note taped to the pillow." On the pillow is a second note: "Vacuum the living room. Then read the noted taped to the handle." Taped to vacuum handle: "Look in refrigerator." A note there says "Take out the trash." On the trash can is taped a note: "Good job. You're done!"

✽Terrific Tacos

Each family member fixes one item for the tacos: shreds cheese, cuts up lettuce, dices tomato, or browns the hamburger.

✽Sundae Sunday

Everyone makes his or her own sundae on a Sunday afternoon. This can become a family tradition!

✽Down Memory Lane

Get out family picture albums and look through them together.

*Giant Board Game

    a. From a cardboard box, cut and tape together a cube. Make dots with a marker to resemble a die.

    b. On sheets of paper, write instructions: *Go back one space; lose a turn; roll again; go back to start; and so on.*

    c. Lay game spaces in any design on the floor.

    d. Cans from your cupboard can be used as playing pieces.

*Paper Sack Puppets

Each family member makes a sack puppet with markers or crayons, using construction paper and yarn for adding features. A simple puppet stage can be made by standing behind a table or hanging a curtain from a spring curtain rod in a doorway.

After your family has enjoyed one of these activities together, close the session with a brief Bible study and prayer. The "One Anothers of Scripture" that follow are appropriate for this family time together. Choose one topic. Allow participation by family members through reading the scriptures, asking questions, or offering insights. Read Col. 3:12-17 together as a family.

One Anothers of Scripture

1. **LOVE ONE ANOTHER**—John 13:34-35; 15:12-13; Rom. 13:8; 1 Thess. 3:12; 4:9-10; 1 Pet. 1:22; 4:8; 1 John 3:11, 16-18, 22-23; 4:4-7, 11-12, 19-21; 5:2; 2 John 5-6.

2. **ACCEPT ONE ANOTHER**—Rom. 14:1; 15:7.

3. **SERVE ONE ANOTHER**—Mark 10:43-45; Luke 22:26-27; Gal. 5:13; 1 Pet. 4:10-11.

4. **BUILD UP ONE ANOTHER**—Rom. 14:19; 15:2; Eph. 4:15-16, 29; 1 Thess. 5:11.

5. **SEEK ONE ANOTHER'S GOOD**—1 Cor. 10:24; Gal. 6:10; Phil. 2:4.

6. **ENCOURAGE ONE ANOTHER**—1 Thess. 3:2; 4:18; 5:11; Heb. 3:13; 10:25.

7. **CARRY (BEAR) ONE ANOTHER'S BURDENS**—Gal. 6:10; Phil. 2:4.

8. **LIVE IN HARMONY AND UNITY WITH ONE ANOTHER**—Rom. 12:16; 15:5-6.

9. **SUBMIT TO ONE ANOTHER**—1 Cor. 16:15-16; Eph. 5:21.

10. **HAVE CONCERN FOR ONE ANOTHER**—1 Cor. 12:25; Phil. 2:20.

11. **BE PATIENT WITH ONE ANOTHER**—Eph. 4:2; Col. 3:13.

12. **FORGIVE ONE ANOTHER**—Matt. 6:14-15; 18:21-35; Mark 11:25; Luke 17:3-4; Eph. 4:32; Col. 3:13.

13. **BE AT PEACE WITH ONE ANOTHER**—Mark 9:50; Rom. 12:18; 14:19; 1 Thess. 5:13; 2 Tim. 2:23; Heb. 12:14.

14. **BE KIND TO ONE ANOTHER**—Eph. 4:32.

15. **DO NOT LIE TO ONE ANOTHER**—Eph. 4:25; Col. 3:9.

16. **DO NOT GRUMBLE AGAINST ONE ANOTHER**—Phil. 2:14; James 5:9.

17. **PRAY FOR ONE ANOTHER**—James 5:16.

18. **DO NOT PROVOKE ONE ANOTHER**—Gal. 5:26.

QUESTIONS FOR DISCUSSION OR REFLECTION

1. Can you think of ways to make this transition easier for your children?

_____

_____

_____

2. If you aren't holding regular family meetings now, how do you think family meetings might be beneficial to all members of the household?

_____

_____

_____

3. What might be a good topic for your first family meeting?

_____

_____

_____

4. Are you and your spouse making it a point to take time to spend just with each other? With your children?

_____

_____

_____

8
Organizational Hints

*Getting your life arranged in an orderly way
will result in additional time.*

You've probably heard the phrase "running around like a chicken with its head cut off." I never really understood exactly what that meant until I visited relatives once when I was a young child. Forever implanted in my memory is watching my uncle chop off a chicken's head and toss the body on the ground, and then watching that headless body run around the yard!

If you're going to be a caregiver and you don't have a system in place, you may find yourself running around from one responsibility to the next—like a chicken with its head cut off.

Everyone has 24 hours to use each day. But it's how you use those 24 hours that will determine your effectiveness. You may have heard the old adage "Some people count time; others make time count." The psalmist prayed, *Teach us to number our days and recognize how few they are; help us to spend them as we should* (90:12, TLB).

Do you often feel pressured by time? It could be that you're either doing the wrong thing or you're doing the right thing in the wrong way. Getting your life arranged in an orderly way will result in additional time. Following are a few ideas to help you save time, organize for efficiency, and make life easier.

Daily Care Plan: The Daily Care Plan on page 85 will help you set important priorities for caring for your aging parent, give you a complete picture of the necessary routine, and make it less complicated for someone else to relieve you periodically.

Health Insurance Record: Consistently filling out the Health Insurance Record form on page 87 will save you hours of time.

Medicine Chart and Medical History Chart: The Medicine Chart and Medical History Chart on pages 89 and 91 will save precious time at doctor's appointments or in case of a medical emergency.

Menu Planning: Talk with all family members living in your home about their favorite food dishes. Then set up the Monthly Meal Planner for lunch and dinner using the form on page 93. Breakfast is easier and does not need to be included in this plan. Use this outline each month to save time in meal planning.

Online Grocery Shopping: Check out Webvan (www.webvan.com) and Peapod.com (www.peapod.com), both of which offer home delivery in selected cities. Also, LifeSpring Home Nutrition (www.homenutrition.com) sells nutritionally fortified freeze-dried foods designed specifically for seniors.

Paying Bills and Filing Insurance Claims: Take a look at the services offered by the American Association of Daily Money Managers (www.admm.com) and the Alliance of Claims Assistance Professionals (www.claims.org).

Home Safety Checklist: Use the form on page 95 to conduct an annual safety check of your home.

Gifts: It can be very difficult to find a useful gift for an elderly person. On page 97 are some ideas for gifts that senior adults appreciate.

Easy Access of Supplies: For parents who are immobile or can't get around easily, keep often-needed items within easy reach, including eyeglasses, books, water, and toilet articles. Keep medical, personal, and cleaning supplies in the room where they're used. Keep a running list of items that need to be replaced so it will be handy on your next shopping trip.

Record of Telephone Numbers: Write down telephone numbers as you look them up, and keep them in an address book, Rolodex, or appropriate file. Taking the time to record the number now will save you time down the road.

The local telephone directory has useful information that should be recorded. This list might include the American Red Cross under Crisis Information, Visiting Nurse Association under Health Services, and items listed under Senior Citizens Services.

The yellow pages of your telephone directory will have information under headings such as Home Health Services, Nurses, Nursing Homes, Senior Citizen Service Organizations, and Social Service Organizations.

Large Crisis-Information Chart: Use a medium felt-tipped, black pen to make a large crisis-information chart for aged parents. Print the letters and numbers at least an inch high so it will be easier for your parents to read, and list all the numbers they might need to call in a hurry. Arrange the numbers in alphabetical order: ambulance, doctor, electric company, gas company, hospital, plumber, police, yourself, other relatives.

In addition to the names and numbers, also print what should be said in case of an emergency. As an example: "This is Elizabeth Benson. I live at 50 Oak Street. I need help." This will help older individuals avoid panic and make certain the emergency service is given correct information. Every second counts in an emergency. Keep a flashlight with charged batteries right by the phone.

Nursing Skills: Having a working knowledge of first aid skills could prove invaluable to you as you care for your loved ones. In most areas, the local community college or American Red Cross offers classes that teach basic skills for home care.

Home Health Care: If your parents need medical care but do not require intensive care, life support systems, or complicated treatment, you may be able to arrange for home health care. This option is rapidly increasing in availability and popularity. Doctors who specialize in geriatric care will be able to recommend individuals or agencies in your area with experience and references in home health care.

Recording Memories: Set aside a specific time in your schedule for recording and sharing memories with your loved ones. This will bring strength to the family and will help the older adult feel cherished and unique as personal achievements are shared.

Scripture says, *Remember the days of old; consider the generations long past. Ask your father and he will tell you, your elders, and they will explain to you* (Deut. 32:7).

A video recording of parents reflecting and reminiscing about the past will have special meaning in the future. If your parents prefer to make a written life review, provide the necessary writing materials or a typewriter or computer. Tape recordings of your parents reminiscing also can be transcribed at a later date.

Locating Help: The evolving electronic explosion means caregiving help remains only a mouse-click away. All major search engines produce answers for key word searches.

The best single information source available for care-giving is the American Association of Retired Persons web site (www.aarp.org).

QUESTIONS FOR DISCUSSION OR REFLECTION

1. Why is time so valuable?

_____

_____

_____

2. How can you make the best use of your time as a caregiver?

_____

_____

_____

3. Do you feel pressured by time? What practical steps can you take in your life to solve this problem?

_____

_____

_____

4. Can you think of other gift ideas for older adults?

_____

_____

_____

5. Which of the ideas in this chapter would you like to put into practice?

_____

_____

_____

9

Legal Issues

Legal issues can be confusing, intimidating, and overwhelming. The psalmist reminds us that *God is . . . an ever-present help in trouble. Therefore we will not fear* (46:1-2).

A lawyer's guidance in preparing a will is well worth the cost.

Last Will and Testament

An estimated two out of three people die without leaving a last will and testament—a written document that directs surviving family members as to how the deceased wants his or her property disbursed. The will names an executor who will be responsible for distributing the property according to the written instructions.

Help your parents understand that it's worth their time and expense to have a will prepared. Otherwise, state law will dictate how and to whom the estate is divided. Putting the names of family members on the back of Mom's and Dad's belongings is not sufficient. A legal services network can be found on the American Association for Retired Persons web site (www.aarp.org).

The will should be stored in a safe place with copies in separate locations and should be reviewed and updated every few years. If a move to another state occurs, the will should be reviewed, since states laws differ.

Contact the planned giving department of your denomination for forms, brochures, and guidance concerning preparing a will. Or use the worksheet made available on the AARP web site. It could save money to complete this form prior to visiting the lawyer.

A lawyer's guidance in preparing a will is well worth the cost. Laws vary from state to state and change over time, and failure to follow all rules and regulations could make a will invalid or difficult to enforce.

Living Will

A living will is a precise directive to hospitals and physicians making known the individual's desires regarding medical decisions should he or she become unable to communicate. It states which treatments are desired and whether pain medication is to be administered once treatment is withdrawn.

Not to be confused with a last will and testament, which disburses the *property* of the deceased, a living will specifies desires regarding the use of life-sustaining treatment in the event of a terminal illness.

Check with your parents' lawyer, health department, or their state's department on aging for detailed and current information on state laws regarding living wills. Some states also require a durable power of attorney for health care.

The terms of the living will should be determined by prayer, godly counsel, and discussion with treating physicians and lawyers and then executed within state guidelines. Copies of the living will should be kept by the lawyer, family member(s), physicians, and other individuals and agencies as directed by legal counsel.

Living Trust

A living trust is a popular concept that enables individuals to transfer their assets into a trust while they're alive. This makes it possible for assets to be bequeathed to family members and others without probate expenses. It can also result in substantial savings in inheritance taxes at the time of death. A revocable living trust is an estate-planning tool that may accomplish what a will won't.

Trust

A trust is a legal agreement whereby title to assets (such as cash, stocks, bonds, real estate, and so on) is transferred to a trustee. The trustee's responsibilities are outlined in the trust document and normally include asset investment, distribution of trust income during the person's lifetime, and distribution of the assets at the person's death. A trust is a supplement to, not a replacement of, a will.

Power of Attorney

The time may come when a parent is unable to handle his or her own affairs. A parent may be incapacitated only in regard to handling financial affairs but is still able to make healthcare decisions. Maybe parents can handle their own daily finances but need assistance with investments. Advance planning will eliminate court proceedings.

Power of attorney documents are inexpensive and easy to execute. A conventional form may be purchased from an office supply store.

Have the document notarized. Planning ahead eliminates the possibility of a parent being sick or unable to sign. Should this occur, call a bank, real estate office, or lawyer for the name of a notary who can go to the parent.

The forms should be witnessed by at least two people, even if not required by law. Witnessing in this way promotes acceptability. It is preferable to ask individuals who are not relatives or anyone who might benefit from the parent's death to serve as witnesses.

LIVING WILL ADDENDUM FOR CHRISTIANS[1]

DIRECTIVE MADE this _____ day of _____, _____, to my physicians, my attorneys, my clergyman, my family, or others responsible for my health, welfare, or affairs.

BE IT KNOWN, that I, _____, of _____, City of _____, State of _____, being of sound mind, willfully and voluntarily make known my desire that if I am in a coma, unconscious, seemingly unable to respond, I request that I continue to be spoken to and treated *as if I could hear and understand.*

I wish to continue to be informed honestly about my condition.

Family, friends, clergy, medical personnel—whoever—please speak *to me* in my presence, not *about me* as if I were not there.

I request that (1) the Bible be read regularly to me, (2) prayer with and for me continue, (3) Christian music and hymns be played for me to hear, and (4) I be informed of ordinary events and news as if I understood.

If I am semi-conscious, paralyzed, or unable to speak, I will make every effort to at least blink my eyes once for "yes" and twice for "no" in response or to squeeze a hand or make a motion to that effect.

If God does not intervene with a miracle of reasonable recovery in answer to earnest prayer, and I am on life support, instruct that such procedures not be continued for a prolonged period. I wish to be released to continue my eternal life in the presence of my Lord and ask that my loved ones rejoice in my promotion. Such a decision is to be made by the one to whom I have given *durable power of attorney for health care,* in consultation with my immediate family.

_____   _____
Declarer   Date

As a witness to this act, I state that I have personally known the declarer and believe said declarer to be of sound mind:

_____   _____
Witness   Date

_____
Address

_____   _____

Witness   Date

_____

Address

State of _____

City or County of _____   SS#_____

Be it known, that the above-named _____
personally known to me as the same person described within and who executed
the *living will addendum* acknowledged to me that said instrument was freely and
voluntarily executed for the purposes therein expressed, and that said *living will addendum* was duly executed in my presence.

_____

Notary Public
My commission expires _____

QUESTIONS FOR DISCUSSION OR REFLECTION

1. What is a will?

_____

_____

_____

2. Why is a will so important?

_____

_____

_____

3. Why is a lawyer's guidance invaluable when drawing up a will?

_____

_____

_____

4. What is the difference between a will and living will?

_____

_____

_____

5. Cite examples when a power of attorney may be necessary.

_____

_____

_____

6. Why is it important to talk with your parents before a crisis occurs to learn their wishes in the event of mental or physical incapacity?

_____

_____

_____

7. Why is it important to know the location of your parents' important documents?

_____

_____

_____

10

Rebuilding Relationships

Forgive as the Lord forgave you.
—Col. 3:13

Beth, a Christian woman in her middle 40s, didn't realize she had harbored hidden resentments against her mother since her childhood until she began to experience the signs and symptoms of physical and emotional stress after her mother moved in with her. As far as Beth was concerned, she had never measured up to her mother's expectations. Her mother, a perfectionist who liked to exercise a strong arm of control, had not provided the hands-on, nurturing environment Beth longed for as a child.

Beth successfully concealed her animosity from herself and her mother until her mother came to live with her. Then unpleasant childhood memories began to surface.

Unresolved anger, bitterness, and resentment are sometimes revealed in a negative reaction when the subject of caring for parents is broached.[1] Painful memories from a past relationship can govern present feelings. If applied to your life, the following scriptural guidelines can be the undergirding for building a bridge to a new relationship with your aging parents.

Jesus said, *If you forgive other people their failures, your Heavenly Father will also forgive you. But if you will not forgive other people, neither will your Father forgive you your failures* (Matt. 6:14-15, PHILLIPS).

2 Cor. 5:17-21 affirms that God's forgiveness gives freedom to love creatively:

> *If anyone is in Christ, he is a new creation; the old has gone, the new has come! All this is from God, who reconciled us to himself through Christ and gave us the ministry of reconciliation: that God was reconciling the world to himself in Christ, not counting men's sins against them. And he has committed to us the message of reconciliation. We are therefore Christ's ambassadors, as though God were making his appeal through us. We implore you on Christ's behalf: Be reconciled to God. God*

made him who had no sin to be sin for us, so that in him we might be-come the righteousness of God.

Adult children and elderly parents are often unwilling to bridge the gap that lies between them. Ask God to help you as you begin your quest to forgive.

Scriptural guidelines can be the undergirding for building a bridge to a new relationship with your aging parents.

Survey the Damage

Nehemiah viewed the devastation of Jerusalem before he designed plans to rebuild:

Then I said to them, "You see the trouble we are in: Jerusalem lies in ru-ins, and its gates have been burned with fire. Come, let us rebuild . . . and we will no longer be in disgrace." I also told them about the gracious hand of my God upon me and what the king had said to me. They replied, "Let us start re-building" (Neh. 2:17-18).

Look inward to survey the emotional damage you have sustained so you can begin repair work. Do you identify bitterness, depression, diffi-culty in loving others, exaggerated attempts for acceptance, fear of rejec-tion, feelings of inferiority, hurt feelings, low self-image, pain, perfec-tionism, inability to trust God, or withdrawal from others?

Who do you feel caused the damage in your life? List those with whom you have experienced conflict, past or present. The list may in-clude your mother, father, or stepparents.

Look inward to survey the emotional damage so you can begin repair work.

Acknowledge the Pain from the Damage

Jesus understands the depth of your pain:

He grew up before him like a tender shoot,
and like a root out of dry ground.
He had no beauty or majesty to attract us to him,

nothing in his appearance that we should desire him.
He was despised and rejected by men,
a man of sorrows, and familiar with suffering.
Like one from whom men hide their faces
he was despised, and we esteemed him not.
Surely he took up our infirmities
and carried our sorrows,
Yet we considered him stricken by God,
smitten by him, and afflicted.
But he was pierced for our transgressions,
he was crushed for our iniquities;
the punishment that brought us peace was upon him,
and by his wounds we are healed.
(Isa. 53:2-5)

We can suffer greatly as a result of painful memories. We pray, *God, change me,* or *Lord, heal the painful memories*—but healing doesn't come. Repressing the pain we feel can actually hinder our healing.

Acknowledgment of pain is a difficult step in the forgiveness process.

At age 41, Cathie realized she was imprisoned in the past. Circumstances from childhood and teen years had caused incredible pain. She had built her own prison, locked the door, and thrown away the key. Although she had been raised in a Christian family, no one at church could have guessed the terror in her home.

When she was three years old, her father said, "If you had been born in China, we would have thrown you in the river." She carried a deep feeling that she was unwanted.

She was often beaten for failure to toe the rigid line. From her seventh-grade year until the end of high school, her father repeatedly abused her sexually. Each time he told her, "I'll beat you within an inch of your life if you tell anybody." Cathie knew he was serious.

After high school graduation, she met a young man, and they married and began their own family. Although the abuse from her father had ended, the guilt and shame often surfaced. Cathie had difficulty establishing relationships and was afraid that if she let anyone get too close to her, the family secrets would be discovered. Finally a Christian counselor was able to help Cathie slowly disclose the nightmare of her past.

God's Word ministered to her. Psalms 25, 31, and 61 became daily bread to Cathie. After following through each step to forgiveness, Cathie shared (paraphrasing Charles Wesley), "My chains fell off; my heart is free. I now go forth to follow Thee." She was ready for service, including caring for her aging parents if God so directed.

Acknowledgment of pain is a difficult step in the forgiveness process. The Holy Spirit brings comfort as painful feelings are courageously expressed.

Some people never gain release from their emotions because they find comfort in feeling sorry for themselves. It's easier to have a pity party or blame someone else than to acknowledge the pain.

Others approach forgiveness casually, declaring, "Oh, I've forgiven my parents." Working through unresolved feelings is hard work, and failing to do so can allow stress-related physical symptoms to accumulate.

Others make the commitment to work through the past, learn to forgive, and gain their freedom.

Write to Release the Feelings

Remember the upsetting incident, feeling, or conflict. Describe it in detail, and write it in letter form. The purpose of this exercise is not to give the letter to the offender—it's simply a method for deep expression to help you release those thoughts and feelings.

Example: "Mother, I feel resentment because you never attended any ballgames when I was in Little League. You had the time. You just always said, 'I don't like baseball.' It made me feel insignificant and worthless. It was humiliating to never have any parental support like the other kids had."

The purpose of this step is to recount incidents and experience feelings so that the poison can be released. This is vital in the releasing process of forgiveness.

Burn the letters. Remember: God has promised beauty for ashes (Isa. 61:3).

List Personal Rights That Were Violated

Webster defines a personal right as something to which one has a just claim. A "right" could be expressed as follows: *I deserve proper nurturing. I deserve praise instead of continual criticism. I deserve being listened to. I deserve time and attention.* List personal rights that were violated:

_____

_____

_____

_____

_____

_____

_____

Yield Those Rights to God

Scripture encourages the yielding of rights:

Yield yourselves unto God, as those that are alive from the dead, and your members as instruments of righteousness unto God (Rom. 6:13, KJV).

A decision of the will is involved: "Do I *want* to let go of these feelings?" If so, your prayer can be, *God, I thought this was a basic right I had. I have clutched it tightly. I now surrender and release it to You.*

List the Wrongs You Have Done to Your Parents

Meditate on these scriptures:

So I strive always to keep my conscience clear before God and man (Acts 24:16).

_____

Your list of wrongs against your parents may include impatience, unforgiveness, or withholding love.

_____

Our conscience testifies that we have conducted ourselves in the world, and especially in our relations with you, in the holiness and sincerity that are from God. We have done so not according to worldly wisdom but according to God's grace (2 Cor. 1:12).

[Keep] a clear conscience (1 Pet. 3:16).

Make your list of the wrongs. Your list may include impatience, insensitivity, insincerity, intolerance, mistrust, pride, slander, unfairness, unforgiveness, ungratefulness, untruthfulness, or withholding love.

What do you think offended your parents the most?

_____

_____

_____

Forgive

When you stand praying, if you hold anything against anyone, forgive him, so that your Father in heaven may forgive you your sins (Mark 11:25).

Bear with each other and forgive whatever grievances you may have against one another. Forgive as the Lord forgave you (Col. 3:13).

Forgiveness seems to be the hardest step. When challenged to forgive, responses often are, "I would like to forgive, but . . ." or "I know I should forgive him [her], but . . ."

Is there anything blocking your ability to love? What's keeping you from forgiving—anger, fear, hurt feelings, insecurity, pride, or stubborn will?

On a sheet of paper write, "My _____ is keeping me from forgiving _____ [name of offender]."

Spend time in prayer with God until you can declare, "I forgive," and there are no "buts" remaining.

Seek Forgiveness

If you are offering your gift at the altar and there remember that your brother has something against you, leave your gift there in front of the altar. First go and be reconciled to your brother; then come and offer your gift (Matt. 5:23-24).

Sincerely asking forgiveness clears the conscience. One approach could be, "I've realized just recently that I was wrong in _____ _____ [describe the offense]. Will you forgive me?"

Desire Reconciliation

Make every effort to live in peace with all men (Heb. 12:14).

Reconciliation does not mean acceptance of what the violator did. It does not mean what happened has to be denied. Reconciliation means the biblical guideline of seeking peace is being obeyed. It is following the scriptural admonition of rebuilding relationships through unconditional love and acceptance.

Love one another. As I have loved you, so you must love one another. By this all men will know that you are my disciples, if you love one another (John 13:34-35).

Now that you have purified yourselves by obeying the truth so that you have sincere love for your brothers, love one another deeply, from the heart (1 Pet. 1:22).

QUESTIONS FOR DISCUSSION OR REFLECTION

1. How does Matt. 6:14-15 apply to your relationship with your loved one?

_____

_____

_____

2. What does reconciliation mean?

_____

_____

_____

3. What does Col. 3:12-15 have to say about forgiveness and relationships with your parents?

_____

_____

_____

4. What do the following verses say about real loving? John 13:34-35; 15:9-14; Rom. 13:9; Gal. 5:14; James 2:8; Eph. 5:28-29.

_____

_____

_____

11
Dealing with Death

I plodded into the house after attending a day-long business meeting. Daddy's light was still on, so I went in for a chat. He stunned me with these words: "Mother and I said our final farewells today. You never know when one of us is going to pass away. Some people die in their sleep. Others just go. So we got that out of the way." I wasn't prepared for the feelings of grief I experienced. I know that all of life is made of seasons, but his words reminded me that the harsh, unrelenting winter was coming, and it was coming sooner that I had expected.

I learned in kindergarten that all living things eventually die. But death is not welcome, and we would all like to hold it in abeyance. Accepting the reality of our parents' death is painful. It forces us to confront our own mortality.

The elderly grasp the certainty of death more readily than the young. It's their adult children who usually want to change the subject or gloss over it. We want to slow the ticking of the clock of mortality, and we're uncomfortable facing our parents' deaths, which break our chain to the past. And when a parent dies, there's no escaping the reality that our generation is next in line.

For many, the presence of our parents in our lives is taken for granted until they become older or ill. But at some point we must accept the fact that they'll not be around forever, and their mortality must be accepted.

Death is not welcome, and we would all like to hold it in abeyance.

We can also help our children prepare for the death of their grandparents. When equipped with the right information, children can usually handle crises. Children under age two will only sense that something is wrong, and they may need extra attention and love. Through age five, boys and girls will not really quite understand and will have many questions. Older children need to know what to expect and what is expected of them.

Fear of death is the most universal anxiety of life. You may want to take time together as a family to discuss what death is, explore everyone's feelings about it, and talk about life after death.

Discussion Starters for Family Time

- What is the inevitable end of the earthly life cycle? Death. Heb. 9:27 says, *Man is destined to die once, and after that to face judgment.* Death is not the end of human existence. See 1 Cor. 15.

- Was death a part of God's original creation?

- Read Gen. 3:19. Death became "natural" only after humanity's first sin.

- If you had a choice, how would you want to die?

- What's the difference between death and dying?

- Which do you fear more—death or dying? Why?

- What do you want to accomplish before dying?

- How did Jesus feel about His own death? Read Matt. 26:36-39 and Heb. 5:7.

- What is the assurance Jesus gives to those who have accepted Him as personal Savior? Read John 3:16.

- Is death the end of life?

Fear of death is the most universal anxiety of life.

Death is seen as final, and endings are painful. Leaving the known for the unknown is not easy, but through the resurrection of Jesus Christ, death has been transformed from an ending to a beginning. Read John 11:25-26.

Scriptures to Read Concerning Life After Death

John 14:1-6	Christ's revelation of heaven
Rev. 21	Description of heaven
Rev. 4	A scene in heaven
Luke 20:27-38	What life in heaven is like
1 Kings 8:30	God's dwelling place
Job 3:17	Place of rest for saints
Ps. 16:11	Place of fullness of joy
2 Cor. 5:1	An everlasting abode of saints

Field Trip

When the death of your loved one is imminent, you might want to call a local funeral home and ask if your family could tour the facilities. Explain that you want your children to see a mortuary so that they're not scared when their grandparent dies and is taken to one.

Planning Ahead

Facing death realistically makes necessary planning easier. Every few months Daddy would say, "Whenever you have time, please bring me the files labeled 'Important Papers' and 'Funeral Arrangements.'" After examining all the items, he would go over it with me again. Outwardly I smiled and was agreeable. Inwardly I groaned, *I don't want to talk about it.* But Daddy's detailed planning greatly decreased the anxiety my husband, my brothers, and I faced when he and my mother died.

Complete the "Funeral Planning Form" on page 99 for both of your parents. Fill in all the blanks as soon as possible to help eliminate unforeseen difficulties later. Careful planning facilitates arrangements.

This organizing also personalizes the funeral. The message, words of remembrance, and style can be tailor-made to fit your parents and conform to their wishes.

Requested Measures of Care

Be aware of terms used by the medical profession:

- **Life Support:** Anything that keeps life going.
- **No Extraordinary Measure:** Nothing is done beyond what is ordinary to maintain life.
- **Comfort Care:** No procedures or treatments are to be done for diagnostic reasons.
- **No Code:** No resuscitative measures are to be taken.

All professionals caring for elderly parents should be apprised of their wishes. Have available copies of living wills (see chapter 6). Be sure correct information is written on all medical records.

A "No Code" sign can be placed as a reminder to emergency technicians as well as physicians. "Comfort Care Only" should be posted also so that no procedures or treatments are done for diagnostic reasons but only to alleviate discomfort.

How to Recognize Death

While Daddy was alive, the morning ritual was unchanged. He awakened before Mother and waited for help out of bed. I tiptoed in, opened the blind, and waited for him to say, "Good morning." I knew that if he spoke to me he was still alive! With no previous experience with death, I didn't know what to expect.

How does one recognize death?

- Eyes are fixed.

- Heartbeat and breathing stop.

- Mouth may be open and motionless.

- Skin turns pale (perhaps blue) and cold.

- After 30 to 60 minutes, the extremities become stiff.

Steps to Take

Procedures to follow vary from state to state when someone dies. Ask the funeral home you plan to use for requirements of state laws. Talk with all family members about the steps that need to be taken. Post the information.

Facing Death in the Hospital

If a parent has only a short time to live and must be hospitalized, talk with the physician about a private room. The final hours should be a family time. Privacy is imperative. Hospitals often allow family members the privilege of round-the-clock time in the room with the patient.

If a "No Extraordinary Measure" decision has been made, be positive a "No Code" is posted plainly on all records.

Politely request items needed to make your vigilant stay comfortable. A cot, extra chairs, pillows, and blankets are useful.

Ask the funeral home you plan to use for requirements of state laws.

Facing Death at Home

A dying parent may choose the comfort of home. When theologian Francis Schaeffer was dying of cancer, he appealed to be taken home, surrounded by familiar things and people he loved. Rather than staring at green hospital walls, Dr. Schaeffer gazed out four large glass panels, enjoying the trees with their first spring leaves. On a continuing basis, the family played his favorite records. He was listening to Handel's *Messiah* when he exhaled his last earthly breath.

Hospice

Hospice care means providing comfort and reassurance to the dying in a peaceful setting. Hospice nurses strive to alleviate pain and reassure fears. Services are provided in special buildings, separate hospital wings, or in the home.

For the nearest hospice address, log on to www.hospicefoundation.org and click on the "Locate a Hospice" button.

When It's Time to Say Good-bye

Jacob's last days are recorded in Gen. 47—50. Knowing death was imminent, he called for his sons, grandsons, and their families and conferred a blessing. This was his spiritual will—his time of summing up and sorting out, passing on the heritage to future generations.

You may want to have Communion together one final time. If so, contact your pastor. What a joy to break bread and drink the cup in the fellowship of the family!

Confirm your love. If your family is not accustomed to openly showing emotions, take the initiative to tell your parent, "I love you." Eliminate at least one of the "I wish I would haves."

"It's Hard to Say Good-bye"

I was concerned when Daddy said, "I wanted to see the performance you're directing tonight, but I'm just too weak." Being his primary caregiver for two years, I had learned to cope with many uncertainties surrounding Parkinson's disease. This was one of them.

Later in the day he had a slight fever, and his breathing became labored. My husband took him to the emergency room for an examination, and I fulfilled my responsibilities for the evening, fully expecting Daddy to be in his bed when I returned home.

My husband returned from the hospital alone. He explained that Daddy had contracted pneumonia and was in intensive care. For some reason, I didn't equate intensive care with "serious." Sure, he was 83, but he had survived several serious operations. I was confident he would soon be back in his favorite chair in the sitting room.

Three days later, I found myself trying to comprehend the prognosis: "fatal," "little chance," "he has three to five days to live." It was a devastating blow. I wept for my father with the anguish of one whose joy had permanently fled.

I dried the scalding tears. Then, stepping to his side, I whispered, "Daddy, I'm going to miss you. I love you so much."

He replied, "It's hard to say good-bye."

The writer in me resolved to record everything he said from that moment. Conversations were jotted on paper towels, magazine ads, and scraps of paper.

If your family is not accustomed to openly showing emotions, take the initiative to tell your parent, "I love you."

During his lifetime, my father had traveled 1.5 million miles in his line of work. With white-knuckled determination, I vowed we would make this last journey together. The hospital provided a private room. My purpose was to help Daddy die comfortably and with dignity. At times, I felt strangled by the antiseptic smells, the maze of tubes, the foreboding mask, the thumping noise of the monitoring machine. But I seldom left his side.

His final words were "I have never felt so tired." Between morphine injections, I would rub sore muscles, offer cold water, and whisper, "Daddy, I love you," "I'm so proud of you," "You can go now—it's OK."

And then, at 11:15 on a Wednesday evening, I released my father. For 45 years he had been a living presence in my life. Now—a memory of love.

Letting Go

Before Daddy died, I had been holding the hand of a friend whose father was terminally ill. One day the phone rang. There were convulsive sobs. Phyllis whispered, "He's gone."

After verbally soothing her pain, I mailed this note: "That diseased, misshapen, hurting body is gone. The memories, godly inheritance, hope of seeing him again are yours forever. You have no regrets, no misgivings, no 'if onlys.' The heart pain is excruciating; your sense of loss is unbearable. But he'll always be your daddy. Not even death can snatch that away."

A line in Robert Anderson's play *I Never Sang for Father* says, "Death ends a life . . . but it does not end a relationship." When the whirling carousel of grief decelerates, the reality of those 11 words can be grasped. The letting-go process can be the primary caregiver's Mount Everest. Because of the daily involvement and interaction, emotions are deep. My letting-go was not a major stage production but rather a short monologue. *Jesus,* I whispered, *You'll have to take care of Daddy now.* And with a deliberate decision of my will, I let Him become the sole Caregiver.

Guilt can ride piggyback at this juncture. No matter what you did for your elderly parent, you may believe it was not enough. Accept the fact you did your best. Relinquish residual feelings to God. *Let not your heart be troubled* (John 14:1, KJV).

What Now?

After a parent dies, your pastor can walk you through the necessary procedure. Have available your Funeral Planning Form (see page 99).

If extended family members need to make airline reservations, have them inquire about bereavement fares. Many companies realize funerals leave families no time to make advance purchases and will waive restrictions.

If your children are not adults, talk with them about what to expect. Describe the room where the casket will be, what people do when they pay respects, why all the flowers are there, and how long they need to stay.

Younger children need to know their grandparent is lying down in a box called a casket. Explain that he or she will look basically the same but will be lying still, with his or her eyes closed.

Show them that the bottom half of the body is there. It's customary to open the casket only halfway.

Never pressure a child to do anything he or she would rather not, such as touching the body. My children were teenagers when Daddy died, and they had never seen a corpse before. Curiosity prompted them to ask, "Is it OK to touch Grandpa?" They both wanted to see what death "felt" like.

Young children should not be forced to go to the funeral home or the funeral. If they would rather not attend the service, encourage them to express why. They may prefer to live with memories of their loved one. Some parents find a "good-bye gift" helps children realize the finality of death. This may mean helping to pick out the flowers, selecting music for the funeral, or making a special gift to put into the casket.

Closure

For many, death's finality comes at the cemetery. For me, it came at the final memorial service, when I knew the coffin lid would soon be closed. Never again would I see that beloved face I had called "Daddy" for 45 years.

I stood tearfully by the casket. Then my husband gently pulled at my left arm. Everyone was patiently waiting to start the cemetery trip, but I could not move.

Accept the fact that you did your best.

My head told me, "This is just his outer form." But I was attached to the body that had housed my daddy. I finally leaned over and kissed him one last time. "Good-bye, Daddy. I love you." Then, resolutely, I departed.

Give Yourself Time

"Death holds no fear for the Christian" is a familiar phrase you've no doubt heard. I always believed in heaven. But until I held my father's hand through his crossing of worlds, I was apprehensive about death. I had never been around it, and the unknown can be frightening. As I watched Daddy slip from this life into the next, I realized death is simply a transition.

However, months passed before I felt the joy of resurrection. Then the Psalm I had memorized during childhood became reality to me: *Yea, though I walk through the valley of the shadow of death, I will fear no evil: for thou art with me; thy rod and thy staff they comfort me* (23:4, KJV).

Life Goes On

A cut finger hurts until the healing process is complete. A scab forms. Then finally a scar is all that remains. Grief is the deepest wound possible. Like a cut finger, healing occurs in stages, and then it leaves a scar.

The Adult Child and Family Deal with Grief

Grief recovery is a process:

1. Accept the reality of the loss.
2. Deal with feelings:
   Anger—"Why?"
   Guilt—"If only . . ."
   Sadness—"What will I do now?"
   Relief—after extended care-giving.
3. Accept the physical and mental pain of grieving.
4. Believe you will eventually reach a point when you can creatively continue your life.

The Surviving Parent

You may have a dual burden: dealing with your loss and being sensitive to the surviving parent's grief. One sympathy card noted: "I'm especially praying for your mother, who now has as much of her heart in heaven as she does on this earth." Matt. 19:5 tells of a man uniting to his wife and the two becoming one. The remaining spouse in many ways may now feel like only half a person.

Your surviving parent will need time to mourn and sort through the confusion of being alone. This disruption to a stable lifestyle must be handled gently. Spend time with him or her. Allow release of feelings. For one caregiver, it was Mother's Day, 15 months after her father's death, before she realized she was expecting her mother to fill the gap left by her father's death. The unrealistic expectations she had of her mother hindered the grieving process for both.

Grieving has no specific time limit. Studies on grief such as those by Elizabeth Kubler-Ross in her book *On Death and Dying* show phases that may be experienced:

Denial—protective device that allows for slow acceptance

Numbness—devoid of feeling

Disorganization and forgetfulness—may come and go

Anger—at a loved one for leaving

Guilt—over things you neglected to do

Depression—normal and usually passes with time

Acceptance—willingness to create a new lifestyle

Awareness of grief stages can bring comfort in knowing your experience is not unique

Watch for these normal responses to grief:

1. Change in sleep patterns
2. Apathy—lack of emotion or interest in life
3. Loss of energy
4. Loss of appetite
5. Deterioration of health and personal hygiene
6. Feeling of hopelessness
7. Dwelling on the past
8. Hibernation—withdrawing from normal activities

Your surviving parent will need time to mourn and sort through the confusion of being alone.

Help your surviving parent make the transition from married to widowed life. Encourage the following:

- The finding of a bereavement companion who can lend a sympathetic ear and give additional support
- Balanced meals plus taking vitamins if nutritional supplement is needed
- Creative routines, different from what the couple experienced together
- Keeping in touch with old friends
- An activity while eating, such as listening to music, watching television, or reading a book
- Keeping active
- Ministry to others

QUESTIONS FOR DISCUSSION OR REFLECTION

1. What does the Bible tell us about life after death?

_____

_____

_____

2. Why is saying good-bye emotionally as well as verbally a crucial part of grieving?

_____

_____

_____

3. How do people deny the death of a loved one?

_____

_____

_____

4. What can be done to help a surviving parent deal with the loss of a spouse?

_____

_____

_____

For More Information

Administration on Aging

The Administration on Aging's web site (www.aoa.dhhs.gov) includes a directory of federal and state services for the elderly in the United States. If you live in another country, your government may have services similar to this and to the following ones. Check them out.

CareQuest

For consultations with a geriatric care manager, one can try the popular CareQuest service (800-327-7138; www.benefitselect.com). For a fee, professionals offer helpful advice and make recommendations.

Children of Aging Parents

Children of Aging Parents (800-227-7294) offers information, referrals, and support groups for caregivers.

Eldercare Locator

The Eldercare Locator web site has information on how to locate the nearest area agency on aging and a wide variety of community services to support older adults: 800-677-1116. www.aoa.gov/elderpage/locator.html

National Association for Home Care

The National Association for Home Care web site includes a checklist to use when selecting a home care worker. The Home Care/Hospice Agency Locator contains a comprehensive database of more than 22,500 home care and hospice agencies. Use this resource to find all the agencies in any area of the country. www.nahc.org

National Association of Professional Geriatric Care Managers

Professional geriatric care managers can be particularly helpful when you're trying to provide care across the miles. They can assess your parent's condition, acquaint you with local services and residential facilities, and recommend solutions in keeping with everyone's financial resources. You can get a list of managers at their web site (www.caremanager.org) or by writing the group at 1604 N. Country Club Rd., Tucson, AZ 85716.

National Adult Day Services Association

The National Adult Day Services Association has a directory to help search for quality community adult day services. www.nadsa.org

National Council on Aging Benefits Check-Up

A free service to help older Americans and their families identify state and federal assistance programs. The service is confidential and takes only a few minutes to complete. www.benefitscheckup.org

National Family Caregivers Association

The National Family Caregivers Association's web site and newsletters allow caregivers to share experiences and swap solutions (800-896-3650; www.nfcacares.org).

State Health Insurance Assistance

State Health Insurance Assistance programs help sort through medical bills. Visit www.medicare.gov and click on "Helpful Contacts."

Forms

Normal wake-up times: _____

Assistive devices needed: ☐ glasses ☐ hearing aid ☐ dentures ☐ cane ☐ walker

Bath time: _____ Procedure: _____

_____

Eating times: Breakfast _____ Lunch _____ Dinner _____

    P.M. Snack _____

Any special eating difficulties:

    ☐ Needs assistance ☐ Difficulty chewing ☐ Difficulty swallowing

    ☐ Special utensils used: _____

Exercise time: _____ Routine: _____

_____

Toileting routine/schedule: _____

_____

Times/channels of favorite TV programs:

_____ _____

_____ _____

_____ _____

Times/stations of favorite radio programs:

_____ _____

_____ _____

_____ _____

If bedfast, times to rotate positions:

_____ left side _____ back _____ right side _____ up in chair

_____ left side _____ back _____ right side _____ up in chair

Usual bedtime: _____ Preferred amount of covers: _____

_____

Preferred nightclothes: _____

Time/dosage of medications:

Medication	Dosage	Time(s)
_____	_____	_____
_____	_____	_____
_____	_____	_____

Date	Service Rendered	Amount Charged	Amt. Billed Medicare	Amt. Billed Supplemental	Amt. Paid Medicare	Amt. Paid Supplemental	Amt. Not Reimbursed That You Paid

- Update this chart after each doctor visit.
- List both prescribed medications and over-the-counter preparations.
- Draw a red line through any medications that are discontinued, and date them.

Name of drug	Dosage	To be taken at	Prescription number	Date started

Name: _____

Mother's maiden name: _____

Date of birth: Month _____ Day _____ Year _____

Blood type: _____

Social Security number: _____

Medicare number: _____

Medicaid number: _____

Secondary insurance name: _____

Address: _____

Phone: _____

Policy number: _____

Known food allergies: _____

_____

Known drug allergies: _____

_____

Date and reason for all hospitalizations (as an adult):

_____   _____

_____   _____

_____   _____

_____   _____

_____   _____

Past medical problems:

_____

_____

_____

_____

_____

_____

_____

_____

Notify in case of emergency:

Name: _____ Phone: _____

Name: _____ Phone: _____

MONTHLY MEAL PLANNER

Number your recipe books. Write recipe book number in parentheses and recipe name on the line.

Day	Noon	Evening
1 ( ) _____	( ) _____
2 ( ) _____	( ) _____
3 ( ) _____	( ) _____
4 ( ) _____	( ) _____
5 ( ) _____	( ) _____
6 ( ) _____	( ) _____
7 ( ) _____	( ) _____
8 ( ) _____	( ) _____
9 ( ) _____	( ) _____
10 ( ) _____	( ) _____
11 ( ) _____	( ) _____
12 ( ) _____	( ) _____
13 ( ) _____	( ) _____
14 ( ) _____	( ) _____
15 ( ) _____	( ) _____
16 ( ) _____	( ) _____
17 ( ) _____	( ) _____
18 ( ) _____	( ) _____
19 ( ) _____	( ) _____
20 ( ) _____	( ) _____
21 ( ) _____	( ) _____
22 ( ) _____	( ) _____
23 ( ) _____	( ) _____
24 ( ) _____	( ) _____
25 ( ) _____	( ) _____
26 ( ) _____	( ) _____
27 ( ) _____	( ) _____
28 ( ) _____	( ) _____
29 ( ) _____	( ) _____
30 ( ) _____	( ) _____
31 ( ) _____	( ) _____

HOME SAFETY CHECKLIST

- [ ] Working smoke detector on every floor, including one near parent's room
- [ ] Well-secured handrails on both sides of all stairs, inside and out
- [ ] Light switches at both the bottom and the top of stairs
- [ ] Steps marked that are especially narrow or have risers that are higher or lower than the others
- [ ] Edges of outdoor steps painted white to be seen better at night
- [ ] Stairways clear of objects
- [ ] Carpet firmly attached to steps along stairs
- [ ] Adequate lighting on all stairs, inside and out, so that each step, particularly the step edges, can be clearly seen
- [ ] Rough-surfaced adhesive strips in bathtub
- [ ] Well-secured towel racks
- [ ] Nonslip bath mat (preferably wall-to-wall carpeting)
- [ ] Two unbreakable grab bars in bathtubs and showers (one attached to structural supports in the wall and one attached to side of tub)
- [ ] Hair dryers, shavers, and curling irons unplugged when not in use
- [ ] Hot and cold taps labeled
- [ ] Hot-water heater turned below 120 degrees to prevent burns
- [ ] Plastic drinking glasses
- [ ] Heavy pots and pans kept on lower shelves
- [ ] Safety caps on all household cleaning agents
- [ ] Nightlights in bedroom and bathroom
- [ ] Lamps or switches located close to each bed (rearrange furniture if necessary
- [ ] Furniture arranged to decrease obstacles
- [ ] Abrasive material such as sand added to porch paint for better traction, especially on ice
- [ ] Tripping hazards removed:
    - [ ] Scatter rugs, runners, and mats
    - [ ] Threshold stripping
    - [ ] Electric cords and telephone wires
    - [ ] Carpet tacked down or with double-faced adhesive tape applied

Remember to recheck your home every year.

- Airline ticket

- Bible on cassette

- Change purse for those who purchase a daily newspaper, use a bus, or pay for doing laundry

- Instant coffee, tea bags, instant hot chocolate, instant spiced cider, or small juices

- Favorite food items

- Fresh flowers

- Fruit arranged in a small basket

- Gift certificates for the beauty shop, a favorite restaurant, or store

- "Labor coupon" for someone to wash windows or do minor home repairs

- Large-print books

- Gift subscription to a favorite magazine

- Original artwork by children or grandchildren

- Photo albums or collage frames

- Stamped envelopes with return address already on them

- Stationery (lined) or postcards

- Telephone certificates

- Envelope or jar with money designated for telephone calls to family

- Tickets to a musical or sporting event

- Updated pictures of family

FUNERAL PLANNING FORM

Full legal name: _____

Social Security number: _____

Legal residence: _____

Place of birth: _____ Date: _____

Father's name: _____

Place of birth: _____ Date: _____

Mother's maiden name: _____

Place of birth: _____ Date: _____

Educational degree: _____ Institution: _____

Educational degree: _____ Institution: _____

Educational degree: _____ Institution: _____

Name of spouse: _____

Place of marriage: _____ Date: _____

Names of children:

_____   _____

_____   _____

_____   _____

_____

Employers:

_____ Dates of employment: _____

_____ Dates of employment: _____

_____ Dates of employment: _____

_____ Dates of employment: _____

_____ Dates of employment: _____

Awards: _____

_____

Veteran Information if applicable:

Which branch: _____ Which war? _____

Discharge date: _____ Serial no.: _____

Location of discharge papers: _____

Honors: _____

Location of will or trust: _____

Safe-deposit box no: _____ Located at: _____

Location of safe-deposit key: _____

Checking acct. no: _____ Institution: _____

Address: _____ Phone: _____

Savings acct. no: _____ Institution: _____

Address: _____ Phone: _____

Savings acct. no: _____ Institution: _____

Address: _____ Phone: _____

List of credit cards and numbers:

_____   _____

_____   _____

_____   _____

_____   _____

_____   _____

Religious affiliation: _____

Minister's name/phone: _____

Address: _____

Lawyer's name/phone: _____

Address: _____

Executor of estate/phone: _____

Address: _____

Medicare number: _____

Medicaid number: _____

Insurance policies: _____

Company	Address	Phone	Policy Number	Face Amount

If funeral expenses have been prepaid:

Plan or policy number: _____

Name/phone number of company: _____

Address: _____

Location of information: _____

If funeral expenses have not been prepaid:

Suggested name of funeral home: _____

Phone: _____ Address: _____

Buried or entombed at what cemetery: _____

Location: _____

Own space or crypt number? _____

What type of service?

☐ Memorial service without body present

☐ Service with body present and everyone welcome to attend

☐ Service with body present and only close family and friends attending

Service to take place at: _____

Address: _____ Phone:_____

Suggestions of person to officiate:

_____ Phone: _____

_____ Phone: _____

Suggestions for musicians:

_____ Phone: _____

_____ Phone: _____

Suggestions of person to read eulogy:

_____ Phone: _____

_____ Phone: _____

To be included in the service:

Music: _____

_____

_____

Scripture: _____

_____

_____

Other: _____

_____

_____

Suggestions for pallbearers:

_____ Phone: _____

_____ Phone: _____

_____ Phone: _____

_____ Phone: _____

_____ Phone: _____

_____ Phone: _____

_____ Phone: _____

_____ Phone: _____

Casket:

☐ to be open for viewing before the service   ☐ to be open during the service

☐ to be open only for close family and friends   ☐ to be closed at all times

Kind and color of flowers for casket:

_____

Memorial gift to be sent in my memory to:

_____

_____

_____

_____

Relatives and friends to contact:

Name: Relationship: Phone:

_____

_____

_____

_____

_____

_____

_____

_____

_____

_____

_____

_____

_____

_____

_____

_____

_____

Notes

Chapter 1

1. *In the Eye of the Storm,* Max Lucado, 1991, W Publishing Group, Nashville, Tennessee. All rights reserved.

2. "Aging Parents and Children Together," www.ftc.gov/bcp/conline/pubs/services/apact

Chapter 3

1. From the poem "Changing Seasons," by Barbara Shaffer, unpublished. Permission granted by Barbara Shaffer. All rights reserved.

2. Marilyn Hamilton, "Full Circle," *Parent Care* newsletter, August 1992. Used by permission. All rights reserved.

Chapter 4

1. From material supplied by Sharlene Pritchett Wade. Used by permission of Sharlene Pritchett Wade. All rights reserved.

Chapter 5

1. "Character Qualities," *Advanced Leadership Guide.* Copyright 1978 by Institute in Basic Youth Conflicts. Reproduced by permission of Institute in Basic Life Principles.

Chapter 6

1. Dotsey Welliver, "Laughing Together" (Elgin, Ill.: Brethren Press, 1986), n.p.

Chapter 7

1. From material supplied by Sharlene Pritchett Wade. Used by permission of Sharlene Pritchett Wade. All rights reserved.

Chapter 9

1. Used by permission of Leona Choy. All rights reserved.

Chapter 10

1. Some of the concepts in this chapter are adapted from materials presented by the Institute in Basic Life Principles. Used by permission. All rights reserved.